Traits of a Winner

The Formula for Developing Thoroughbred Racehorses

Carl A. Nafzger

The Russell Meerdink Company
Neenah, Wisconsin U.S.A.

Library of Congress Cataloging-in-Publication Data

Nafzger, Carl A., 1941-
  Traits of a Winner: the formula for developing Thoroughbred racehorses.
  Includes bibliographical references and index.
  ISBN 0-929346-32-7: $34.95

1. Race horses--Training.   2. Thoroughbred horse--Training.   3. Race horses.   4. Thoroughbred horse.   I. Title.
SF351.N34   1994
636.1'32--dc20   94-35092
                                                              CIP

Published by:

The Russell Meerdink Company, Ltd.
1555 South Park Avenue
Neenah, WI 54956 U.S.A.
(414) 725-0955
Printed in the United States of America

Dedicated to Mrs. Frances A. Genter
and her love
for the uniqueness of the
Thoroughbred

Acknowledgments

When I entered into the agreement to write this book, one provision in the contract concerned me. The publisher insisted on assigning an editor/writer to help organize the project and put it in a format appropriate for publication. Although it was never quite stated. I knew the job of this "editor" was also to keep the pressure on to get the job done in a manner that was acceptable to the publisher. I had dealt with writers before and frequently what I really said to them - or meant to say - was not what appeared in print. It would be an understatement to say that I was less than enthusiastic over the intrusion of this "editor" in the affairs of putting together this manuscript.

Les Sellnow, a frequent contributor to the *Blood-Horse* and the *Thoroughbred Times* and the past editor of *The National Show Horse,* was assigned as my editor. It took a few sessions before we started to get to know each other. Little by little, I came to realize that - unlike dealing with the press - Les was devoted to helping me tell my story in the way I wanted to tell it, not necessarily the way someone else wanted it told.

Les is an accomplished and successful horseman himself. Over time, my suspicion turned to respect and finally to friendship. His suggestions, help and skill with words appear on every page of this book. Wanda and I will be forever grateful for his help and we look forward to a lasting friendship with Les and his wife Linda.

The thanks to the many people in the Thoroughbred world is endless, but especially to all those in the early years: H. L. Armstrong, John and Norma Morris, Ray Bell, Tom Bell.

Also to all those special friends who have gone on before us: Mrs. Genter, Dean Pavillard, D.V.M., and John Swann.

This book would not have been possible without the faith and trust of the many owners and their horses throughout the years, the help and friendship of my fellow trainers and mentors especially John Nerud, the personnel of Broken N Stable and the whole community of people who devote their lives to the Thoroughbred. I thank you all for being part of it.

To the photographers who chronicled the Unbridled years - Robin Berry, Caren Goodrich, Dan Johnson, Suzie Oldham, Steve Stidham, Jean Raftery, Shegeki Kikkawa, Leslie Martin and ABC Sports - and allowed us to use their work - and Les Sellnow, who recorded the day-to-day work of Broken N Stable. . .thank you all.

None of this would have come about without the encouragement of Jim and Gus Tafel and my publishers, The Russell Meerdink Company, Ltd. - Russell, Todd, Jan and their staff.

And the most important "thank you" of all - to Wanda Raye, who was always there and kept picking up the pieces and putting them back together again.

Carl A. Nafzger

As you believe, it shall be.

Table of Contents

Chapter One

Understanding the Horse

Some people claim that any damn fool can train a racehorse and they may be right.

Successful trainers come in all stripes. One's level of formal education isn't important. There's no school that can teach you how to get a horse physically and mentally ready to bolt out of a starting gate. Thoroughbreds don't care about your background, nor do they care about your lifestyle. A racehorse won't penalize a trainer for the way in which he or she lives, unless, of course, that lifestyle interferes with getting the horse mentally and physically fit for a race.

Anyone can train a racehorse - but they will only become successful if they really learn to understand horses.

The successful Thoroughbred trainer and the successful coach of human athletes have a lot in common. Take a coach of a professional football team. Success on the football field starts with recruiting raw talent. The coach must find the best athletes available and select from that pool of talent those players who exhibit the traits of a winner.

But recruiting talented players with winning traits isn't enough. The coach must understand the personality and quirks of each player. Each must be treated as an individual. Some must be worked hard and disciplined frequently to bring out the best. Others must be treated gently and with much praise so their spirit is not broken. The success of the winning coach lies not so much in getting the muscles of talented players fit, but rather in getting their minds ready to win. A team with the best talent in the world will never win the championship unless its coach has the understanding and ability to motivate and develop that championship talent.

It's the same with training Thoroughbreds. No matter how good a trainer may be, he isn't going to win the big race unless he has a horse with the talent and other traits to be there in the first place. And the trainer who doesn't understand horses won't win the big race even if he has the best horse in the world.

What I'm saying is that to successfully train a horse for a career on the track, one must come to know and understand that horse as an individual, not as just another unit to which some "written in stone" training method is going to be applied. If one can combine knowledge of the basics with an understanding of equine psychology on a horse-by-horse basis, then a training program rooted in sound, common sense will have strong potential for success. The dream of the football coach may be to win the Super Bowl, but his real role is to develop each athlete to play up to the level of his ability. The dream of the trainer may be to win the Derby, but his role is also to develop each horse to compete up to the level of its ability.

When speaking of training there is one important point that must be understood. No one can literally train a horse to run. The horse will run because that is its nature. It learned way back in the early days of its existence that flight beats fight. The trainer's task is to make certain that the horse is in a healthy frame of mind and that its body is finely tuned so that it can take the best possible advantage of the ability with which it was born.

To accomplish that, the trainer must have learned to know and understand that horse and to have adapted his training methods to meet the horse's physical and emotional requirements. Anybody can learn the ABCs of training, but it takes time, mental effort and a real desire to get inside that horse's mind to, first of all, understand it and then adapt training techniques to accommodate the animal's physical and emotional needs.

Adjustment.

You're going to read with frequency in the following pages about adjusting. I don't mean the horse's ability to adjust to a certain regimented training program. I mean adjustment on the part of the trainer and everyone else connected with the horse. You can establish on paper or in your mind the most logical training program in the world for a horse, but if it is unhappy or uncomfortable in that regimen, it will be unsuccessful because the horse will not perform to the best of its ability. And, if a horse is not performing to the best of its ability, it not only isn't going to win very many races, but it may also pick up a number of destructive bad habits in the process. When that happens, you become burdened with a horse that is a liability instead of an asset and that, in turn, is detrimental to owner and trainer as well as racing in general.

There are a thousand ways to train a racehorse, but there is only one finished product at the end of a training program that will bring success. That finished product is a horse that is happy, confident, relaxed and responsive to what the rider asks of it. If the horse is happy, confident and relaxed, it will eat well, it will rest when in the barn and, most importantly, in the excitement and drama of a race, it'll go through a hole and battle for the lead when the jockey asks it to. It will be a horse that does not make mistakes.

Of course, just being happy, confident and relaxed doesn't guarantee a stakes winner. I'll get into more detail on this later,

Before we can begin training and racing, however, we

11

must first find the horse we are seeking. Success on the racetrack begins with finding a horse with the traits of a winner. There's no way to be sure that a horse has those traits just by looking at him. Only after putting him on the track and studying how he performs can you make a determination whether or not he has the traits of a winner.

There are four traits which are essential for a horse to become a winner :

1. Ability.
2. Mental toughness.
3. Soundness.
4. An excellent immune system.

Ability: Obviously, ability or talent is the number one requirement when you're looking for a winning racehorse. It's easy to define ability. Simply, a horse that can run faster and farther than most has the ability to be a winning racehorse. If a horse is born with only the ability to compete at the $5,000 claiming race level, it doesn't matter what training methods you use or how well you understand it, you aren't going to turn that runner into a stakes contender. On the other hand, if you have a horse with stakes ability and fail to understand its physical and emotional needs, you can reduce it to a $5,000 claimer in short order.

While it's easy to define ability, it is not so easy to spot in the untried horse. A horse inherits its level of ability and later I will discuss how I try to find it in a young horse. But until you get a horse to a track, you are never certain whether he has it.

Mental toughness: A winning racehorse must be mentally tough. Training and racing impose a great deal of stress on every horse. Although the role of the trainer is too reduce the level of stress on the horse, it can never be eliminated entirely. Winning horses can stand up to a reasonable amount of pressure and stress. They can endure the aches and pains of training, the stress of new situations and the pressure of competition. The losers just seem to fall apart under the slightest amount of stress.

Unfortunately, horses by their very nature are not "mentally tough" creatures. Their nature is to flee from stressful situations rather than stay around and deal with the circumstances. Mental toughness in horses is relative. To be successful, a racehorse must have more mental toughness than the average horse. But even the horse which has a higher level of mental toughness must have as much mental stress eliminated from its life as possible.

Mental stress is the one factor over which man has a great deal of control. You can't give the horse ability, you can't make it sound if it's unsound and you can only partially control the immune system. But, a trainer plays a major role in preventing most forms of mental stress and in teaching the horse to cope with different forms of stress - such as pressure and tension before a race - that can't be eliminated. If a trainer has the right handle on preventing or coping with a horse's mental stress, this in turn, will have a profound effect on maintaining a strong immune system, which also is reflected in remaining sound and definitely is involved in keeping a horse mentally fit.

There are so many ways we induce unnecessary stress in racehorses. Sometimes it starts with observing what might only be a minor physical problem, say with a back leg. You don't want to stop training for a race you're shooting for, so you kind of gloss over the problem and pretend it isn't there and keep pushing forward. Pretty soon you don't just have a low tire behind, you probably have a flat up front because the horse tried to do what you asked, but compensated by transferring additional weight to the front end. You stressed the horse mentally and physically and the stress led to unsoundness.

In a case like that, it's much better to back off the training regimen even if it means you miss a planned race. Solve the basic problem first and then move on with the program.

Understand the horse and its needs and adjust to them.

Over-matching a horse regularly also produces harmful mental stress. Let's take our $5,000 claimer as an example. If you put it in top allowance company, it very likely is going to get soundly defeated. Don't think horses don't know when they get soundly beaten. They do and it will ultimately have a detrimental effect on attitude.

It's kind of like putting an Olympic level boxer against Mohammed Ali in his prime. You can tell that Olympic boxer how good he is and get him all pumped up to fight Ali. When he gets soundly whipped, he's going to begin doubting everything he's been told. You might be able to talk him into a return engagement, but if the same thing happens again, the biggest battle you're going to have before the third bout is getting him out of the locker room.

You run a horse that isn't mentally or physically ready, or against higher-class company than it can handle, and the same thing is going to happen with it. Pretty soon that horse isn't going to want to go to the paddock and once there, it doesn't want to leave. It becomes nervous and agitated on the way to the starting gate, which it doesn't want to enter, and ultimately runs a lousy race. Everybody is a loser - the horse, owner, trainer and the fans who bet on it.

Sometimes debilitating mental stress is induced right in the horse's stall. If a horse is going to reach and maintain that razor sharp level of physical fitness and mental well-being, it must be happy where it spends most of its non-racing time. A good example is a filly that came into the barn. She was an immediate problem because she laid her ears back and snapped at any horse that went by in the shedrow and was doing the same to people who came near her. Worst of all, it had a negative effect on her training program. I knew there was some kind of mental stress factor involved and it had to be understood and solved if we were going to have any success with her.

In studying this filly's attitude as I got to know her, I realized that what she needed was her own space - her own privacy. I put up a screen in front of the stall door instead of just the normal webbing. Though it was a screen that she could see through, it provided the feeling of privacy and the comfort zone she was craving. She no longer felt a need to defend her territory.

The change in her attitude was dramatic. She relaxed and ignored the horses being walked past her stall in the shedrow. She became mellow with her groom and, best of all, there was a complete turnaround in her training attitude.

Putting up the screen was such a simple thing and it solved the problem. Had we dismissed her attitude as being simply that of a spoiled or ill-dispositioned horse, she likely would have gotten more sour both in her stall and on the track and that would have resulted in a filly not performing to her ability.

Stress.

It's something a trainer must understand and deal with in a positive manner. If he doesn't, stress can compromise everything else being done in the attempt to get that horse ready for a successful racing career.

Soundness: The winning racehorse must be sound. Muscles, bones, ligaments, tendons, and cartilage must all hold up to the physical stress of training and racing. Ability, mental toughness and a good immune system aren't worth much if the horse doesn't stay sound. It's like owning a race car. The fastest car in the world isn't much good if it has a flat tire.

One of the important roles of the trainer is to make sure that the horse is not put under undue physical stress. Since horses are individuals, some can endure more physical stress than others. Knowing when to back a horse off of training is important. But no matter how careful a trainer may be, some horses just seem to be injury prone. It's one thing right after another. The plain truth is that some horses just stay sound while others can't be kept sound no matter what you do.

A good immune system: Look around your work place. Some of your co-workers seem to catch every cold, flu-bug and virus that goes around. Not only do they seem to be susceptible to every "germ-of-the-month" but whatever they catch seems to impair their ability to function. They always seem to be missing days at work because of an illness. Other of your colleagues never seem to come down with a cold or the flu or if they do, it doesn't seem to bother them much. Their missed days of work because of illness are infrequent and of a short duration.

It's the same way with horses. A horse moves from farm-to-farm, track-to-track. At each new location there are new bugs in the air. Some horses seem to catch the bugs at a drop of the hat. The great ones never seem to catch anything, or if they do, they shake the bug quickly.

A horse's ability to stay healthy is in large part due to its immune system. It may also have something to do with its mental toughness. Doctors now tell us that human health is part mental. I'm sure that may also be the case with horses. But whatever it may be, some horses will never get to perform up to their potential because it's impossible to keep them healthy enough to do so.

I've mentioned ability, mental toughness, soundness

and a strong immune system as necessary ingredients in a winning racehorse. There is another element that is a must.

Class.

Class wins horse races.

Class welds everything else together. It is that elusive element that enables a horse to overcome adversity - including trainer and jockey errors, poor track conditions, tough competition, the worst gate position and getting bumped at the start - and still win.

Unbridled had class. It was class that kept him from making mistakes in a race. Unbridled did not make mistakes in any of his races. His trainer did, his jockeys did and his owners did, but Unbridled made no mistakes. I've trained a lot of horses, but none better than Unbridled. He won the Kentucky Derby and the Breeders' Cup Classic, earning more than $4 million in his racing career.

Class.

You can't define it in concise terms and usually you don't know for dead certain whether a prospect has it until you put that horse to the test on the racetrack. When you own or train a horse with class, you enter a world of satisfying excitement like no other. There will always be lows in this precarious world of horse racing, but if you have a class horse competing, the highs will completely overshadow them and lift you to heights of excitement you've never before experienced.

Let me make one thing crystal clear. The class horse we dream about owning and training may not be the one who has the ability to win the Kentucky Derby and Breeders' Cup as Unbridled did. Instead, it might be that $5,000 "Secretariat" that you come to love and enjoy just as much because it never lets you down. Running against its peers, it will be the horse that always gives 110 percent and will relish doing battle with all comers in its ability group.

If you love horses and horse racing as owner or trainer you must have the ability to love that horse with the same fervor, devotion and attention to his well-being as you do the ability-favored Unbridleds or the real Secretariat.

Whether dealing with a Derby contender or a $5,000 claimer, there is no "secret method" or training approach that will insure success. Instead, the goal of the trainer must be to understand that horse as an individual and then adjust basic conditioning and training techniques to satisfy its needs.

Before we can begin training and racing, we must first define why we want to be involved in horse racing in the first place and what it is we want out of this exciting sport.

Chapter Two

Charting the Unknowns of Ownership

Involvement in horse racing opens the door to an exciting new world which can be lucrative if approached in a businesslike manner. However, before one invests money, time and emotion, two questions must be answered:

1. Why am I getting involved?
2. What do I expect to get out of horse racing?

Honest answers to those two questions will serve as a guide in everything that follows for a prospective new owner.

When examining answers to the question of why people want to get involved in Thoroughbreds and racing, one generally finds that they do so for a couple basic reasons. Maybe they were around it as kids with their parents and want to return; maybe they have a friend who is involved and want to feel the same excitement their friend does on race day, or maybe they just simply love the sport for the challenge and want to have some fun at the same time.

There is another mystifying attraction and maybe it is the most intriguing of all.

The unknown.

Successful business and professional people, generally speaking, are successful because they have eliminated most of the unknowns they face on a daily basis. They know how to bid a contract, prepare a case for trial, make the right moves at the right time in the financial market, buy when prices are right for their retail outlet or whatever it is in which they are involved.

In racing they are perhaps returning to the same type of unknown challenges they faced with getting started in their own business or profession. And believe me, racing is a world filled with unknowns. Just about the time you think you've got it all figured out, a $7,500 colt comes along and runs second in the Derby. The Thoroughbred is a great equalizer and also is capable of humbling the proudest of owners and trainers.

Racing is full of stories about the million dollar colt that couldn't run and the one, like Casual Lies, which sold for $7,500, that could.

The unknown.

You guess, you theorize, you analyze, you prepare, but you still don't know for sure what's going to happen race by race until the horses reach the finish line. That is what creates excitement, enthusiasm and keen anticipation in racing. There is the old cliché that you never hear of an owner committing suicide when he or she has an untried two-year-old coming up.

The world of the unknown also touches the financial aspect. I have always maintained that Thoroughbreds are the greatest and most exciting speculative investments in the world. You might give $10,000 for a horse and it might turn out to be worth zero. But, you also might give $10,000 and wind up with a horse that's worth $500,000.

That same kind of speculative excitement doesn't exist in the purely financial world for most people. It exists with Thoroughbreds because we're dealing with a living, breathing animal filled with courage and a desire to be a winner.

The Thoroughbred can carry one to heights of excitement and recognition never realized before in life and they can also plunge one to the lowest depths of despair. However, even the lows have their own value because they make the highs that much sweeter.

20

If the answer to the question of "why" is an unemotional one - such as getting involved with racing just to make money and nothing more - that person is letting himself or herself in for some serious disappointment and a totally unsatisfying experience. One has to love the sport to enjoy it and be a success. If one does, then the definition of success changes. While you continue to approach racing as a business, it becomes a business with many satisfying elements. You aren't just counting dollars in purse winnings. Instead, you are also getting a wonderful high when your horse makes that electrifying move in the home stretch and wins or at least runs to the peak of its potential.

Once the question of "why" is answered satisfactorily, it is time for the new owner to become involved with what amounts to a key sub-contractor - a trainer he or she can trust.

If the relationship between owner and trainer is to be a successful one, it must contain two very solid and essential ingredients - communication and honesty. If there is communication and honesty in the relationship from beginning to end, most everything else will take care of itself.

That relationship should begin with a frank discussion about what the new owner expects and can afford. The worst thing a trainer can do is to convince a new owner who can afford to pay the costs on three horses, to have five in training. This sometimes happens when there is early success with one of the first horses and purse money helped pick up the tab for training. At this point it's pretty easy to convince a new owner that if he had five horses instead of three in training, the odds of winning would be increased. In this scenario good can turn to bad in a hurry. Maybe one of the five comes up with a bad ankle, another has a foot problem and another just can't run. Now, the owner with a $6,000 monthly budget is facing expenses of $10,000 and getting little in return.

He is unhappy because his dream has been taken away

and replaced with a financial headache. He is probably spending money on racehorses that he needs for paying the kids' college bills. He has been robbed of his excitement and anticipation. Nothing's left but the worries about meeting bills. Before long that owner will be out of racing. Nothing sours a new owner on racing faster than investing more than he or she can afford.

This doesn't mean a trainer should become a financial adviser. Definitely not. That is a job for the owner's accountant. The trainer's obligation is to make certain the new owner knows exactly what financial obligations must be faced. Armed with that knowledge it is up to the owner to then tell the trainer just what the level of involvement should be.

Honesty and communication.

Trainers should make it clear right up front to new owners that unless one is going the claiming route, a racing investment does not produce overnight returns. At whatever level the new owner chooses, he or she ought to be prepared to handle predicted expenses for several years.

The trainer has a major obligation to keep the owner informed about what's going on. The biggest mistake many trainers make is that they only call the owner when something's wrong. That owner has invested money in a horse and has entrusted its care and race preparation to the trainer. The owner has a right to know on a regular basis how his investment is doing, not just when a calamity occurs.

That does not mean the trainer should be on the phone with a report on every little incident, good or bad, in training. But, it does mean that if, for example, the trainer realizes a horse lacks the potential to meet the owner's expectations, either as the result of injury or lack of ability, the trainer has an obligation to let the owner know right up front, not after a lot of money has been spent to prepare for races the horse won't be able to run.

The trainer has a major obligation to keep the owner informed. The owner has a right to know on a regular basis how his investment is doing, not just when a calamity occurs.
Photo by Les Sellnow.

Most trainers are tired after spending a day at the track. When they get home at night they just want to kick back and relax. That's when they must summon up the energy to give the owner a call, particularly if the horse did something well that day. Maybe he hit the desired fractions in a work that had earlier been discussed and targeted. The owner should share in the excitement of that training accomplishment. He or she will then feel an integral part of the team.

A trainer shouldn't pump up the owner and tell him that every horse he has in training is the greatest racer to set foot on the track. That's dishonest. Instead, the owner should be fully informed about the horse's rate of progress and what, generally speaking, to expect from it in the near future.

One rule that I've always followed is never to call the owner immediately after an injury occurs. I am not talking about a life threatening injury where the owner should be informed immediately, but the kind that might keep the horse out of racing and training for a time. If you call before you know the extent of the injury and what it means in terms of lay-up or recuperation, you wind up talking about a lot of negative unknowns because you aren't sure what the injury is and you don't know what you're going to be able to do about it.

It is better to wait until the horse has been thoroughly examined by a veterinarian, x-rayed, or whatever else is required in the diagnosis. When those results are all in, I feel I'm in a position to explain exactly what happened, discuss the prognosis and outline what this may mean in terms of the owner's investment. This call might be made 18 or 19 hours after the injury occurs, but I'll be able to answer the owner's questions and provide some solid information concerning the horse's future.

Honesty and communication.

If there is honesty and communication between owner and trainer, the owner will also keep his expectations within the level of investment. This does not mean the owner shouldn't dream of winning the Kentucky Derby with his colt or filly, but he or she should not live in expectation of that happening and be disappointed when it doesn't. In other words if the owner buys a colt for $20,000 and it turns out to be an exceptional individual that can really run, have a good time and truly enjoy it. But, if it doesn't turn out to be an exceptional runner, the owner should be happy and satisfied if it runs to the best of its potential at its ability level.

If both owner and trainer approach racing with that type of honest attitude, it will save them from disappointment and prevent the horse from being over-matched because somebody is dreaming the impossible dream. It's much the same as your feelings for your own children. You want your son or daughter to be the best player on the field, but one day

24

you realize that he or she is only average as an athlete. When that's the case, the greatest disservice you can do is to push that kid to a level of competition that is over his or her head. That son or daughter will be a lot happier being involved at a level where he or she is competitive. Or, maybe their real interest is in something like playing the piano instead of basketball or baseball. (Some Thoroughbreds have no desire to compete in a race, but make excellent jumpers, dressage competitors or trail horses.)

If a horse has the ability to compete well as a $20,000 claimer, that's where it ought to run, not in an allowance race where it doesn't belong and might be destroyed mentally.

If the owner can't appreciate that $5,000 "Secretariat" then he or she ought not to be involved with horse racing.

It is the trainer's obligation to help teach the new owner to respect what the horse did in a given race, particularly if it put forth its best effort, no matter where it finished. I tell owners that you can't expect to win all the time. If they want to truly enjoy racing, they must learn to enjoy the effort their horse has given them.

Back when I was just getting started as a trainer and struggling to make ends meet, a man I knew sent me five horses for which he had great expectations. It was obvious to me right up front that these horses weren't capable of living up to those expectations. Yet, someone who had this man's ear had convinced him that all five were top-notch runners that could win. As a result, he wasn't going to enjoy hearing about or watching his horses run unless they could win.

One of the five was a colt that he had bought for lots of money and from which he expected great things. He had been told the colt had great potential. I was told when I got the colt that he was about ready to run, but he wasn't. All that was needed, I was told, was to get the colt approved for the starting gate. I put the colt in training and worked him out of the starting gate. He didn't handle it very well, though he received his 'ticket' (starter's approval). It was obvious to me that this colt was not ready for a race.

I called the owner and told him so.

He said, "Well, he is too."

I said, "Okay I'll enter him, but he isn't ready."

He wasn't ready and lost by 25 lengths.

The man was a good friend and at first I didn't know what to do, but finally I realized that being totally honest and straightforward was the only way to handle it. I called him and said I was sending all of his horses home. I had only nine horses in training at the time, so to lose five out of the barn was a big hit.

He could not understand why I was sending the five home. I told him that I would rather be his friend and be able to have a cup of coffee with him than to keep horses in training that I knew couldn't meet his expectations and would result in the end of our friendship.

We stayed good friends and later he sent me another horse and this one could run and did win. But, the point remains, unless the owner can enjoy his horses within the limits of their ability, everybody is going to be a loser.

When a new owner comes aboard, the role he or she is to play and the role the trainer plays should be clearly defined immediately.

Even when the roles are defined and understood, there will always be that occasion where the two won't see eye to eye. Again, I can give a personal example. An owner put a colt in training with me. As his training progressed, I learned that the colt didn't have much ability and told the owner so. He was disappointed and said that another trainer told him he had watched the colt work and knew for certain he could run. I said the colt surely had not shown that kind of ability to me and I was convinced he couldn't be a winner.

At this point the owner had invested about $18,000 in training and it was time for him to cut his loss. I tried to tell him that it might hurt now to have someone tell him the colt couldn't run, but that it would hurt a lot more to have it confirmed after he'd invested another $15,000 or $25,000 in training. He decided I was wrong and the other trainer was right. He took the colt out of my barn and placed him with the trainer who told him what he wanted to hear.

The owner called me about a year later, saying he had another horse he'd like to send. He said this about the previous horse: "You're right, it did hurt a lot more to find out my colt couldn't run after I'd spent another $20,000 on him."

The key point is that the man now knew I had been honest with him and though my honesty caused him to send that colt to someone else who either was being dishonest or truly didn't know, the end result was I had a clear conscience and the owner later wanted me to train a good horse for him.

At the same time, the trainer must also remember he isn't God. The best of trainers can be wrong. If, however, the trainer is totally honest with his advice, the trainer-owner relationship will be strong enough to weather any temporary setbacks. The trainer should also remember that it isn't his job to *tell* the owner what to do. His job is to *advise* and then step back and let the owner *decide*.

Most owners have already been successful in their chosen field and don't want to be totally responsible for the success of a venture they're entering for enjoyment. Instead, they are looking for what amounts to sub-contractors who will help them make a purchase, care for the horse on a daily basis and train it for the end result - racing. Most people who get involved are willing to pay the bills and share the excitement, but the last thing they want is to be responsible for every little decision that must be made.

However, because they've been successful in their own

endeavors, they also don't want to be passive players. They want to be involved in the decisions of what horse to buy, where to buy it, where it should be raced. (It doesn't make much sense, for example, for an owner who lives in Chicago to have his horses racing in California. If that particular owner is going to truly enjoy the horses, they ought to be raced in the Midwest so that he and his family and friends can see them run and share in the excitement.)

There has been a distinct change in ownership ranks in recent years and, in my opinion, it's a change for the better. One of the key reasons for this change is the Tax Reform Act of 1986. Before '86, there were a lot of what I term "paper tigers" in the horse racing business. These were people with no real love for the Thoroughbred or the sport of racing. They were merely taking advantage of the tax laws and used Thoroughbreds and racing as tax write-offs and nothing more.

I remember being at a sale one time when a fellow who fits into the "paper tiger" category came up to me.

He asked, "Carl, where do you board your broodmares?"

I said, "I don't have any broodmares."

He was shocked. "You don't have any broodmares? Man, that's where all the money is. In broodmares."

I said, "Yeah, I guess so, but I only have racehorses. Do you have any horses running?"

His reply: "No, I don't have any racehorses. You have to be a damn fool to actually race them."

This man didn't care about Thoroughbreds. He was breeding horses and taking the money of anybody who'd buy them, but he didn't care about racing. All he cared about was the money he could put into his own pockets. That kind of person was not good for racing and, when they were swept away by the 1986 tax change, I said, "Good riddance."

Fortunately, the foundation farms and families in racing, those who had been involved for years, stayed the course. They have continued to breed Thoroughbreds and have prepared the products of those breedings to do what they are best equipped to do - race.

The new owners that have followed in the wake of the "paper tigers," are, for the most part, people who love Thoroughbreds and racing and, at the same time, approach this venture as a business. I don't have a single owner in the barn today who doesn't approach racing as a business.

They ask tough questions. They want to know what is going on and why. They are the greatest people to deal with because they know that, though it's a heady world filled with emotion and excitement, it isn't a bowl of cherries. They know that it is a business with business decisions to be made, and not all of them will be the right decisions. They want to be informed with honest, accurate information.

Honesty and communication.

It does wonders for the relationship between trainer and owner and that is healthy for racing in general.

Now, that we have taken a look at why people get involved in racing, it is time to take a deeper look at what specifically they expect to get out of it.

Is it quick action the new owner wants? Is it immediate involvement? If so, a potential owner might want to examine the claiming route. You can get involved in a hurry with claimers. A horse that is claimed might be getting a start for its new owners three weeks later. The downside risk is less with claimers, but upside potential is restricted.

For example, if you claim a horse for $25,000, you might be able to move it up to the $30,000 claiming ranks, but that is about all you can expect to accomplish because, generally speaking, the horse's trainer is going to have it competing at its ability level. An owner can expect quick action with claimers, but should not expect miracles. Where the horse is in class when you buy it, is about where it will be when you send it to the starting gate the first time or, later, when someone else claims it.

The upside is that a new owner can get into racing quickly, maybe make some money, get out quickly, and do it all with a modest investment.

Maybe a potential owner is someone who would love to breed horses and watch them develop under another person's ownership and training. If that is the case, they should be looking for fillies or mares with excellent pedigrees and locate top-notch stallions for breeding. They will get their thrills when the colt or filly brings a good price in the sale ring and, perhaps, later when it is a success on the track for its new owner.

Of course, everyone who has a Thoroughbred would also love to own the horse that wins the Kentucky Derby. If a new owner sets out with that as the prime goal, however, he or she must be prepared to assume some serious financial risk and suffer disappointments. Remember, of all the Thoroughbreds born each year, only a tiny handful will ever start in the Derby and only one of them will win it.

Instead of setting forth to get our hands on that Derby winner, let us take a look at what is involved in getting into horse racing by buying a quality yearling or two at one of the Thoroughbred sales. First, about $40,000 to $50,000 will be required to make the purchase. Then, you have to assume that developing the yearling into a competing racehorse will cost about 80 percent of that particular purchase price. This means a buyer must be in the position to set aside another $32,000 for paying the bills through early summer of the horse's three-year-old year. That cost will be constant. Only the percentages will vary, depending on the amount paid for a particular yearling. If, for example, $200,000 was paid for the yearling, the $32,000 in development costs would be a lower percentage of purchase price.

The goal is to start the horse competing, at least lightly, at two and continue with a full-fledged campaign at three. By the end of the horse's three-year-old year, the owner should have made the decision to either keep it as a racehorse, hopefully as one that he or she can go all the way with because it is winning and making money or, if ability level so dictates, running it in claiming races, hoping to win a few purses before someone else becomes the owner. If the horse has no real ability, it should be dropped way down in class in claiming races and wait for someone else to take over paying the training bills.

The point is that by the time the owner has reached May or June of the three-year-old year of a yearling purchased for $40,000, the grand total investment will stand at about $72,000. Hopefully, that has been augmented by winnings, but when making that initial $40,000 purchase, a person should be prepared for a $72,000 investment.

Again, we come back to honesty and communication. The trainer working with a new owner should take it as a personal obligation to get that person into the racing business in such a way that he or she will still be involved years down the line.

There is much more to be said about a trainer's relationship with owners, but let's talk next about what's involved in getting a prospective new owner into the Thoroughbred racing business in a way that will enable him or her to stay the course, enjoy the emotional highs of this great sport and, at the same time, be a benefit to the industry.

Chapter Three

Buying at Auction

Buying a Thoroughbred yearling at auction is a heady experience, but it is also something that requires time, knowledge and a strong team effort. There are so many parts that make up the whole picture of what we are looking for that it's about impossible for one person to do it alone.

The team should consist of the owner, trainer, pedigree analyst and veterinarian. The owner comes first. He or she must take an honest look at expendable resources and decide how much can be spent initially and how much is available for the long term.

It's time for realistic expectations. It does little good to thoroughly examine a horse's pedigree and conformation and decide it is just the one you want when you know it will sell in the $100,000 range and you have only $40,000 with which to make the purchase.

Again, I come back to those two absolutely necessary ingredients at this point - communication and honesty. The owner and trainer must be on the same wave length as to available funds, commitment to a plan and expectations before the rest of the team goes into action.

Let's go back to the scenario we discussed earlier where the owner decides he or she can spend $40,000 for a yearling and also is prepared to come up with the $32,000 as developmental cost over the next couple years. Now that we have that established, we can begin our search in earnest.

Pedigree.

I like to approach pedigree from two viewpoints - long-term family traits and also what I call "racehorse pedigree". You will want an expert to research this horse's family background as to what the genetics have demonstrated through the years concerning the passing on of desired traits. This must be a person with in-depth knowledge about a wide variety of bloodlines and who knows how well one has crossed with another through the years. You will want to know from that person about female lines and which mares have been good producers and which have not. When you find lines that consistently pass on desired traits, follow them.

You want to know the genetic strength of the stallions involved and how certain sire lines nicked (crossed) with certain mare lines. The pedigree expert should provide you with a broad overview or genetic map for where you're going.

Later, when studying that report, you will come to realize that you shouldn't waste time on certain horses because they either will be beyond the $40,000 price range or they come from family lines with poor performance records.

Each of the two pedigree studies - genetic and "racehorse" - is equally important. You may, on paper, have the greatest bloodlines in the world, but paper doesn't win horse races. You have to know more about the specific family being considered. The dam of one of the yearlings, for example, may have super bloodlines, but if she herself has had eight foals and not one of them is a runner, chances are the ninth one won't be a runner either. If she has been bred to good stallions and hasn't produced anything good in eight tries, you have to assume that she never will and her offspring should be removed from your list of possible purchases.

What you're looking for from the dams at this point are females who may not have produced world beaters, but whose foals are runners and have won somewhere between $60,000 and $100,000. You must remember that you are not shopping for a Derby contender as such. You are looking for a yearling in the $40,000 price range that has a good shot at becoming an allowance winner and, if you are lucky, might even graduate into the stakes ranks. And, if you get even luckier, and catch "lightning in a bottle" and have a Derby contender, so much better.

"Racehorse pedigree" comes into play with some specifics. You want to know where the runners competed, against what kind of competition, whether they raced only at two and then retired or whether they stayed sound and were still running at three and four years of age.

All along the way you are attempting to locate something else in the pedigree analyses.

Dominance.

All horses have a trait or traits that dominate no matter how they are crossed. This does not mean that every offspring of that mare or stallion will be born with that specific trait, but it does mean that percentage-wise, the majority will. The traits can be good or bad. A dominant trait may be for soundness or it may be for unsoundness. It may be for nervousness or it may be for a quiet disposition. It may be for intelligence or it may be for a questionable temperament.

Percentages.

Our goal is to determine the positive dominant traits in stallions and mares that parented the yearlings we're considering and then calculate how often these traits have been demonstrated in the offspring. We are looking for a high percentage mark in soundness, disposition, intelligence and, of course, ability.

Sometimes the percentages can take some weird turns. There are, for example, in some family lines, horses of a particular color that do well and others of different colors that do not. Why or how that happens, I don't know, but it does happen. It might be a case of where the bay offspring in a certain family line won't run, but the grays will. While there is no logical explanation, I have had personal experience that convinces me this is a factor to be considered in the selection process.

The same is true of general conformation. In some lines, the lanky horses can run and the more muscular ones can't or vice versa.

I had a horse from a prominent family line that trained well and was a winner. He was a bay. All the chestnuts from that same family were horrible on the track. They all looked good. They were pretty and had good basic conformation, but not a single one of those pretty chestnuts amounted to anything as a racehorse.

The successful bay from that family would have to be described as ugly when compared to the chestnuts. Same family, same high percentage marks for soundness and ability, but just not pretty. But, the bay could run. We wound up running him in Grade I stakes and he won $400,000 during his racing career.

Percentages.

Always look at the percentages.

As with everything else in racing, there are exceptions to every rule. Once in a while you can breed the sorriest stud to the sorriest mare and produce a stakes winner. However, the percentages definitely aren't in your favor when you try that. Racing is a game of percentages as much as anything else and you must learn to use them to your advantage

A question that has been and, I guess, always will be debated is whether the stallion or the mare has the greatest influence on the traits a foal inherits. I believe that, generally speaking, the mares will dominate. If I have a mare that has proven she passes on positive dominant traits a high

36

percentage of the time, I don't worry too much about the stallion as long as he is at least average or above. On the other hand, if I have a stallion with a lot of dominant positive traits and he has been bred to a mare with very few, I get concerned about their offspring.

It gets a little more complicated when you are studying yearlings from young stallions and mares who as yet have no production records. At this point you have to go back to what they did themselves on the track as well as determine what were the dominant traits in their sires and dams.

My way of approaching the pedigree analyses of a yearling purchase is this: I have a pedigree expert study the family backgrounds of each of the horses being considered. At the same time, working independently, I do my own analysis from the "racehorse pedigree" approach. When we both have finished our analyses, we compare notes. The horses that are going to get strong consideration from here out are the ones that show up on both of our lists with a positive report.

Now it is time to actually go to the barns where these yearlings are housed and look at the horses we've targeted. But before we do, there is another factor that deserves serious consideration.

The consignor.

You want to deal with consignors you know and can trust; the ones who have always been honest with you. That does not mean you have to know every single consignor, but it does mean that you should at least know them by reputation. As much as possible, you want to deal with people who have a reputation for accurately representing their horses. If you have had positive personal experience with them, so much the better.

These will be consignors who, in case some problem crops up after the hammer falls, will work with you to solve it. They will be the type of people who won't try to cover up a fault or injury just to get the yearling through that particular sale session. Most consignors are honest, but like with everything else, there are exceptions.

In a sense, that consignor, if he or she is honorable, becomes a fifth member of your team of owner, trainer, pedigree analyst and veterinarian.

Our narrowing down process has continued. Now, we are at the barns prior to the sale. We know from pedigree which horses we're interested in and we've checked to determine who is consigning them. It is time to consider another very important element.

Conformation.

Chapter Four

Checking Conformation

The great trainer, John Nerud, a man who has taught
me so much, used to say: "Don't go to a stakes paddock to study
textbook conformation."

Some of our best stakes winners have conformation
'faults.'

Books on correct conformation are good, but what they
teach does not always apply to racehorses. The horse that
passes a strict conformation inspection might not be able to run
a lick while another with obvious faults might be a stakes
winner.

This does not mean we ignore conformation. Far from
it. It means that when we look at conformation we do so in the
context that it's part of the whole picture, not the entire
picture.

There are some conformational faults that are very
unforgiving. If, for example, you buy a yearling with a
misshapen knee that does not permit the proper distribution of
concussion from the ground up through the withers, chances
are you are going to have soundness problems in training and
racing.

However, there are other faults that aren't so serious.
Unbridled had feet that would have caused a lot of
conformation experts to raise their eyebrows. One foot turned
out a bit and the other turned in, but neither was serious. We

always joked that at least they both pointed in the same direction.

Unbridled won more than $4 million on those feet.

That being said, the fact remains that conformation deserves serious consideration as long as we don't approach it as though it alone is what matters.

The conformation examination begins when you see the horse being led from the barn. We are looking for a horse that walks straight and true. Watch it as it walks. Is it pigeon toed where both toes point in? Is it splay footed where they both

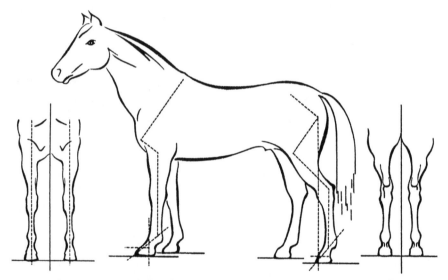

A conformation chart can be helpful in determining the ideal alignment of the parts of the horse. No horse is ever perfect, but charts such as this can serve as a guide as you inspect yearlings for possible purchase.

point out? Is it calf kneed where the knee is set back from the cannon bone or is it over at the knee which is the reverse? Is it sickle hocked where the back leg at the hock curves too far beneath the horse's body? Is it cow hocked where the hocks are closer together than the feet? Or, is it wide at the hocks? (I much prefer a horse that is a bit cow hocked to one that is wide at the hocks.)

It's stride should be free and easy at the walk. I want to see a good, solid, aggressive walk, not charging and not gawking around; just a good brisk go-forward walk with a nice, long, free stride.

Now that we've seen the horse walk, it's time to step back and take a hard look at all of the yearling's components. What should strike your eye at this point, if the horse is to fulfill expectations on conformation, is a well-balanced horse. There ought to be symmetry and an alignment of muscles, bones, tendons and ligaments with one part flowing right into the next with no serious deviations to stop your eye as it travels over the horse's body.

Let's start with the feet, one of the most important of the components. You can have the best Cadillac in the world, but you aren't going to travel anywhere if you have flat tires. It's as simple as that. A horse has to have good feet if it is to perform well over the long haul. No foot, no horse. The feet do not have to be perfect, but there are certain things that should be avoided.

You would not prefer what we term a mule-footed horse. This is one with a long narrow foot. This is the kind of horse that has a tendency to come up with contracted (pinched together) heels. When a horse with contracted heels runs, it could be feeling pain from those pinched heels each time the buttress (rear of the heel) strike the ground.

Carefully check the hooves themselves. You prefer not to see any vertical cracks in that hoof wall. However, you or a member of the team should be able to differentiate between serious cracks and sand cracks that may not cause a problem. A horse with vertical cracks that extend into the coronary band and which show signs of causing a defect in hoof growth and development is rarely acceptable.

While you prefer not to see any cracks in the hoof wall, a horizontal crack normally isn't a serious problem.

Look carefully at the farrier work that has been done on this yearling. Has the hoof wall of a pigeon-toed horse, for example, been rasped down to give the illusion that the foot is straight?

I recommend that only an experienced horseman on your team pick up the feet of potential purchases for examination. An inexperienced person can be injured if the foot is picked up improperly. Most importantly, only an experienced horseman will know what to look for once the foot is picked up.

It is better to ask the consignor how best to approach this part of the evaluation. If the horse is being presented outside, it may be a good idea to return it to a stall for a closer examination of the feet.

Is that outside horny wall of the hoof thick or thin? A thick wall indicates a horse with a strong healthy foot. A thin wall will wear down quickly and be subject to cracks. It should immediately raise questions about present and future soundness.

Are there ridges around the hoof? If there are, it is an indication that this young horse has had some kind of infection or other physical trauma which caused a change in the normal rate of hoof growth. Be cautious if considering a horse with growth ridges on the hoof. Find out what happened to the horse to cause their appearance.

Is it a dish-footed horse? This is a foot that, when you stand back and look at it, resembles a duck's bill. This is also a foot with which you likely will have soundness problems once that horse is in training. When you see this type of foot, it is time to call on a veterinarian and/or farrier to provide an expert's opinion. It is also the type of foot that may need to be x-rayed.

You do not want to see a club-footed horse. This is a condition where, in serious cases, the heel of the foot rests on the ground in nearly vertical position instead of at angle that is in alignment with the pastern. This condition can be serious or relatively minor, depending on degree. Horses with a minor club-foot problem can often race successfully, but those with a serious condition will be unable to distribute concussion properly when they run and face the likelihood of being unsound.

You also want to be concerned with the moon-footed horse. This is one with a big, round foot where the sole is too close to the ground. This type of foot will likely have a thin sole without a good cup (the natural concave configuration of the bottom of the hoof). As a result, the sensitive sole is less protected from impact, especially when the horse travels on a hard surface. This will cause the horse to attempt to distribute its weight differently, unbalancing the animal and changing its natural way of going.

You must always remember that the foot is the horse's first line of defense in absorbing concussion when running. Anything that compromises that concussion-absorbing ability compromises the horse's ability to perform at its best and remain sound.

The next line of defense in absorbing concussion is the pastern, that portion of the leg between the hoof and the ankle or fetlock. We are looking for a pastern that is neither too long, nor too short. An overly long pastern will be weak and will put undue stress on ligaments and tendons in the leg and often is a key culprit in sesamoid (the small bones at the rear of the ankle) injuries. A pastern that is too short will not absorb enough concussion and send the shock waves straight up the leg at every stride. The angle should be consistent with the horse's overall conformation.

43

Next we come to the ankle. As you look at this part of the leg from the front, you want to see what appears to be a flat surface. As you examine the sesamoid bones at the back of the ankle or fetlock, you want them to be smooth.

Between the ankle and the knee is the cannon bone. We are looking for a cannon bone that comes out directly

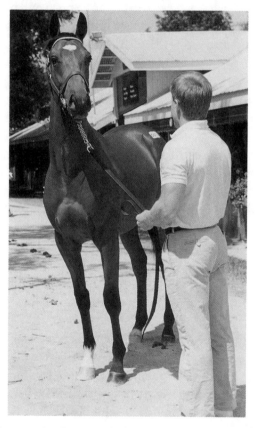

This yearling is "pigeon-toed." Note that both front feet point inward.
Photo by Suzie Oldham

beneath the knee and fits into the middle of the ankle. If this bone is offset one way or another from the knee, it means that bones, ligaments and tendons are not aligned for maximum structural strength. You are going to be facing problems because with every stride taken, force is going to be exerted against a single unaligned point and produce structural weakness instead of structural strength. Concussion must be evenly distributed.

The same is true for the forearm that extends from the shoulder to the knee. It, too, must be in alignment, down through the knee and cannon bone and on into the foot to provide the maximum structural strength through proper distribution of concussion.

Here again is where balance comes in. As you examine a yearling, you do not want to be looking at a cannon bone that is overly long or one that is too short. How do you know if it's

This horse is "splay-footed" - both left and right feet are turned out.
Photo by Suzie Oldham

the correct length? It will be the correct length, if it is in balance with other components of the horse's conformation.

Balance.
Symmetry.
Alignment.

This yearling is base wide. Wide-chested horses generally do not have the proper balance or alignment to become successful racehorses.

Photo by Suzie Oldham

Examine the tendons that run from the knee to the fetlock and into the foot. They should appear strong; flat and smooth.

You want the forearm to blend into the shoulder smoothly. You don't want a shoulder that is straight. It should be laid back at about the same angle as the pastern to insure freedom of movement and the ability to carry out its role as

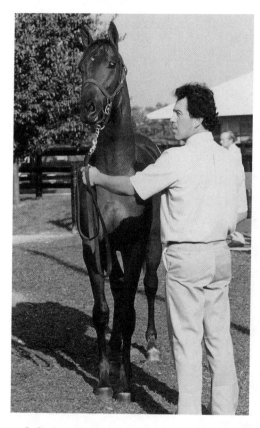

This yearling is "base
-narrow."
Photo by Suzie Oldham

part of the concussion-absorbing mechanism.

When you look at that yearling's chest and shoulder from the front, you're looking for a horse that has a nice V-shaped chest. This is an indication that the horse is balanced, with bones, muscles, ligaments and tendons in proper alignment to provide freedom of movement. If I have to cope with one fault or another, I prefer a horse that is narrow in the chest to one that is too wide. The wide-chested horse just simply isn't going to have proper balance and alignment and, as a result, isn't going to have freedom of movement, nor proper distribution of concussion.

Next, you look at the neck and how it fits into the overall picture. I have never seen a good racehorse with a weak neck. I don't mean that you want a cresty, stud-like thick neck. You want to see a strong, straight neck that fits smoothly into the withers and shoulder.

The head. I'm probably less concerned about heads than anyone I know. A lot of people get hung up on the big-eyed, pretty headed horse. I don't. Maybe the problem is that I've had too many pretty headed horses that couldn't run. I

This yearling is unbalanced in its conformation. It also shows a "nervous eye."

Photo by Suzie Oldham

want to see a good eye on this horse, but it certainly doesn't have to be that big, show horse eye. By a good eye, I mean a horse that looks around alertly, sees what's going on, but isn't rolling those eyes so they show white. The horse with the white showing is often the horse that's going to be flighty and might be difficult to train. However, many horses with this type of eye are good runners.

Before we leave the head, there are a couple other aspects that bear attention. You want to see a good, clean throat latch, that area where the head connects to the neck. If this is thick and coarse, it generally indicates a horse that isn't well balanced. The horse with the clean, slender throat latch not pinched - also is normally the horse whose breathing apparatus is in proper alignment. The same is true of a horse that has ample width between the jowls. Finally, you want to see a horse with broad nostrils, which means it has the capability of getting a lot of air into its lungs when running.

Take a look at the teeth. You want to see good sound teeth that have developed properly and are consistent in their development with the horse's age.

Next, examine the withers, that part of the anatomy where the neck joins with the backbone. You want to see withers that run straight, long and clean.

When looking at this horse from the side, you want to see a long underline. At the same time, you want the back, beginning at the withers and running to the point of the croup, to be relatively short. The horse with the long underline will have a good, long stride, while the short back denotes strength and the presence of a long hip which indicates power.

You want to see a little slope to the croup (the area between the end of the back and the tailhead). You do not want an exaggerated slope. About 10 to 15 degrees is my preference.

When you look at a horse from the rear, you want to see plenty of muscle in that rear end. You want to see a good inner gaskin muscle (the muscle just above the rear hock) that ties in well. That is where I believe the horse gets its real propelling power - from the gaskin.

As you look at the horse from the rear, you want it to be broad across the top of the hips. You want to see muscle definition, which reveals that the horse has a smooth, flat and efficient muscle structure. We are not looking for a horse with huge, bulky muscles because that will do nothing for it except provide extra baggage to carry.

If you don't have a strong rear end on a horse, you can't take care of the front end. To me, the rear end is the most important conformational aspect of a horse.

I believe that the majority of injuries start in the rear end. It's true that most injuries are to the front limbs, but very often they originate in the hindquarters. These injuries wind up in the front because the horse compensates for a rear end problem by shifting weight, pressure and physical stress forward.

Finally, step back and take another look at balance. As you eyeball this horse, does everything fit together? If you think in terms of a circle, beginning at the withers and traveling around the horse's body, do you have a round circle, as you should, or is it oblong because one part of the body or another is not in balance - out of alignment - with the rest?

If you see before you at this final observation, a yearling whose body flows together smoothly and gives the impression of strength, speed, soundness and the ability to remain balanced and coordinated when running, it may be time to mark it down as a possible purchase.

However, now that you've figuratively disassembled and put back together, the yearling being examined, with no serious faults found, there are a couple other final questions that beg answers before you give it that final positive mark in your sale catalog. How about attitude? Is this a calm, confident horse? Does its bearing give you that indefinable feeling that makes you think "class"? Even though this is the umpteenth time it has been led from its stall to be examined, does it still walk off alertly?

If the answer to these final questions is yes, you have one that should be marked in the catalog as a purchase prospect.

This horse has good overall conformation and balance. *Photo by Suzie Oldham*

The question of which is better, the big horse or the little horse is a subject that will always be debated and maybe never answered. I equate it to football players. If one football player is big and the other is small, but they both have the same degree of quickness and desire, the big player is going to have an advantage.

However, I am more interested in a well-balanced horse than in any particular size. Unbridled is a good case in point. He's extremely well balanced. He stands about 16.2 and was a lean, well-muscled horse when he was racing. He wasn't a Mr. Universe, but he wasn't a string bean either. He had a nice, wide, distinctive muscle with an excellent gaskin, just what you're looking for in your yearling prospects. Personally I like my racehorses to range in size from 15.3 to 16.2 hands.

In the wake of your conformation examinations, you'll find that once again you've reduced the number of possible purchases listed in the sale catalog. By now, hopefully, you have a select group of horses that are within the $40,000 price range, have solid pedigrees and good conformation.

It's also a good idea at this point to have the veterinarian give the purchase prospect an endoscopic examination to determine whether there are any breathing problems. With an endoscope, the veterinarian can look into the horse's throat to make certain nothing hinders proper functioning of the epiglottis or any other aspect of the breathing apparatus.

It's getting close to sale time.

You have studied, examined, and studied again the prospects that you are considering. Team members have met and compared notes. Each purchase prospect has been discussed at length. Agreement has been reached on which of the yearlings merit bids.

It's time to head for the sale ring.

Chapter Five

Sale Ring Drama

Sitting through an auction after you've decided to invest in a Thoroughbred yearling can be one of the most exhilarating and nerve wracking experiences of a lifetime. Up to this point, you have graded the prospects pretty much at leisure. The seller has been willing to have you walk around the yearling, lead it off at a walk and even have a veterinarian do some basic examinations.

Once the sale itself begins, all that changes. Things happen in such rapid-fire fashion that it can be overwhelming and unnerving. The average yearling is actually in the sale ring only a minute and one-half to two minutes. This means you must know when to begin bidding and, most important of all, when to stop.

Before all that happens, however, it's time to double check some basics. Prior to the sale, as prospective buyer, you should have applied with the auction company for a line of credit. This means that you must make a decision on just how much you are going to spend and once decided, that is a decision that shouldn't be altered significantly in the heat of bidding competition.

Remember, too, that once the hammer falls and you are the high bidder, you own that horse. If he takes off through the sale ring, into the crowd and out into the parking lot and is struck and killed by a car. That dead horse is your property.

To protect yourself, establish a working relationship

with one of the insurance agents at the auction so that when the hammer falls on your purchase, the animal is instantly covered with mortality insurance. You will want to tell the insurance agent, generally speaking, how many horses you plan to buy and how many dollars you are apt to spend. Make certain that you and the agent understand each other - that when the hammer falls your new purchase is covered.

The worst thing you can do is wait two or three days to get the insurance in force. It takes only seconds for a catastrophe to happen; if it does and you aren't insured, your entire investment is gone.

Once you own the horse, it has to be transported somewhere. It can't stay at the sale grounds after the sale is over, nor would you want it to. By now, working with a trainer or adviser, the decision should already have been made as to where the colt or filly will go for breaking. The trainer or adviser should also know which of the transportation companies represented at the sale handle yearlings in the manner you, as a new owner, will desire and the trainer approve.

Make at least tentative arrangements with them ahead of time so that your newly purchased yearling gets off the grounds and to its new home in a timely fashion.

Before taking your seat in the sale pavilion, there is one other thing that you and your team should have done - rate your prospects by desirability. You might assign the letter A to your first choice, B to the second choice and on down the line.

If you are very lucky, the A horse will be the first one in the ring. Don't count on it. It rarely happens. More likely, your least desirable horse will be the first of your list of prospects to be sold. Having your lowest rated horses sell first presents you with a predicament. What do you do if the horse ranked about 10th on a list of 12 is the first to sell and is going near the price you have decided it's worth? Do you buy or do you wait for one of the higher ranked individuals to come through?

There are no easy answers to these questions, but there is at least one thing you can do that will help in making decisions. I use the rule of thumb that I'm normally willing to give 10 percent more for a horse than the amount set by the evaluation team - if I really like the horse. But, if I don't have strong feelings about a particular yearling, then it does not qualify for the 10 percent above the initial evaluation.

So, if one of the horses further down on your list comes into the ring first, either don't raise your hand or, if you do, raise the bid only to the amount at which your team evaluated the horse and no more.

Above all, don't let yourself get caught up in the excitement of competitive bidding and suddenly realize that you've just paid $65,000 for a horse that your team evaluated at $40,000.

Believe me, it's easy to get caught up in the sale ring excitement as the auctioneer is sailing along with his chant and bid catchers are waving their arms and yelling whenever a new bid comes in. And all the yearlings coming through the ring are in beautiful condition with their coats gleaming and their manes and tails all neatly combed. They will present some serious temptations now that you've made the decision to buy.

Remember this. When that yearling steps into the ring, that's as good as it's ever going to look to you until the day you stand beside it in the winner's circle. It won't look as good in its stall early the next morning as it recovers from the stress of being shown, looked at, led about and finally being taken into a small oval area with sound and excitement all around it. Many a buyer has looked into a box stall the following morning and asked: "Is that really the colt I bought yesterday? I wonder if I paid too much."

Be alert, be ready to bid when one of your prospects comes in, but always contain your excitement. There's plenty time for that after the hammer falls. Now is the time to concentrate on bidding strategy in a calm, businesslike manner.

The auctioneer's job is to get all the money he can for the horses going through the ring. Your job is to buy the horse you want at the price you've decided you can afford, or less. This doesn't make the two of you competitors, but it does mean that you should learn the auctioneer's rhythm and know when he really intends to drop the hammer and when he's just cajoling bidders for more money.

First of all, the auctioneer normally will start the horse at a higher figure than anyone is willing to bid. Sit tight, because in a matter of seconds he will lower that starting price to a realistic level that will stir activity.

At this point you might want to get involved in the bidding competition or you might want to wait until the field has been narrowed down considerably, providing of course, that the bidding is still within your price range at that point.

You only have to raise your finger one time to buy most horses.

I repeat, don't get caught up in the excitement of a bidding war.

Auctioneers are paid to sell horses and they are very skillful at it. If you're strongly interested in a colt and so is someone else, the auctioneer will do everything he can to turn it into a fast-paced competition that will have the two of you raising each other rapidly and with ever increasing amounts. Where moments before you were raising your bid by only $1,000, you suddenly find that you're raising it by $2,000 and then $3,000 increments or even more. One moment you are sitting there with the bid at $40,000 on a colt you evaluated at that amount or maybe even less, and, suddenly, after raising your hand another time or two, you look around and realize, "My God, I just bid $60,000." At that point all you can do is say a little prayer that the other party wants the colt worse than you do and will raise the bid once more. If they do, you heave a big sigh of relief and vow never to get caught up in that kind of competitive bidding again. If they don't and the hammer falls, you own a $60,000 yearling that cost you $20,000 more than you planned to spend.

It is possible that it could turn out to be the best buy you'll ever make, but the problem is that you are just starting a new venture and after owning the horse for only a second, you already have gone over budget.

There is no reason to panic and jump right in on the bidding when your prospect comes into the ring. Before the auctioneer hammers down a horse, you usually have 15 to 20 seconds where he will be asking for one final bid. Let's say a horse we evaluated at $40,000 has reached $38,000 and no more bids are coming in. The auctioneer is going to hang on that number for a short time - sometimes only seconds - before he says "sold." If you've been sitting tight, this is the time to raise that bid by a thousand or whatever amount that seems appropriate. Of course, that does not guarantee that you are going to be the successful bidder. That will be determined in part by the other person who also wants the horse.

If he or she raises the bid to $39,000, you can come back with $40,000, which is what your team feels the horse is worth. If the other bidder raises to $41,000, it's time for some quick decisions. If this is one of your top choices, you might want to invoke the 10 percent rule and carry the bidding to $44,000 or $45,000. If the prospect is in the middle or at the lower end of your list, stop at $40,000 and wait for your next prospect to come through.

Do not expect to become a bidding expert the first time you set foot inside a sale pavilion. It takes some observing and some doing to get it down pat. As the sale goes on, if you're being observant, you will be able to zero in on an auctioneer's rhythm and figure out just what he is indicating with his chant. If you listen for it, you can usually tell, for example, when he is just under a horse's reserve bid and needs another increase in money to get the horse sold.

Reserve bids are established by the sellers to protect themselves from having a horse sell too cheaply. If a breeder has invested $40,000 in stud fees, mare care and the like, he is not going to let that horse sell for $40,000 as a yearling unless forced to do so. Instead, the average consignor will determine how much has been invested, what percentage of profit he desires - he's probably looking at somewhere between 20 and 30 percent profit on his investment - and then set the reserve bid accordingly. Generally, only the consignor and the auctioneer know what that amount is.

If no one bids the reserve amount or better, the auctioneer hammers down the horse as sold, only it goes back to the consignor who pays the sale company the commission on that bid the same as consignors whose horses actually change ownership.

Back to the bidding process. I make it a point to do all of my bidding with the same bid taker inside the sale pavilion. Normally, I don't want everybody in the place to know I am interested in a particular horse, because that might tend to stimulate interest on the part of other people. I establish a discreet signal that the bid taker will instantly recognize because he now knows me and knows how I bid.

Sometimes buyers try to watch what the professionals are bidding on and then jump in because they think the fact that professional buyers are bidding on a particular colt or filly is a strong indicator that the horse in question is a good prospect. When that happens I may realize that the price has just gone up $10,000 because someone else is "chasing" my bid, based primarily on the fact that buyers like myself or certain other trainers are known to completely evaluate a horse before bidding on it. At least some of that can be avoided if no one knows I am bidding.

What you do not want to happen is for someone else to benefit from all of your homework. Your team has made use of years of accumulated knowledge and spent time, effort and money to evaluate the yearling prospects. You do not want someone else, who is your bidding competitor, benefiting from that investment.

I remember being at a sale where I thought I was actually going to buy at a bargain price. The filly in question was the only one in this particular sale that I was really interested in. For some reason the other buyers just were not interested in her. I had myself as hidden as possible and had the top bid at $15,000 which was well below the amount at which our team had evaluated her. At this point, the consignor saw that it was me bidding, surmised correctly that I definitely wanted the filly, and began bidding against me. I eventually bought her for $25,000. She was worth every penny of it and more, but the point remains that when someone else knew I was bidding - in this case, the owner - the price went up.

By the way, I believe this to be a fair approach on the part of the consignor - bidding on his or her own horse. The horse consigned is that person's property and represents an investment. He or she has every right to protect that investment, whether it involves running up the bid as this man did or setting a reserve which, if not met, costs the owner a commission, but allows him or her to train and race the horse or sell it to someone else privately.

I have been on both ends. If I am selling, the horse's value is going to be handled just as though it were back in my barn in a stall. When someone comes to buy a horse privately, I set a price on it and that stands. Either it's met or the horse

59

stays. The same is true in the sale ring. If I have a horse that I think is worth $25,000, there is no way I am going to sit quietly by and let someone else "steal" it for $12,000 or $15,000.

Of course, if a consignor is strapped for cash and has to sell, that is a different story. Sometimes financial circumstances force a sale at a price that normally would not be considered. When this is the case and you are in the right place at the right time, it can result in a bargain purchase.

Personally, I like to be inside the sale pavilion itself to do my bidding. Some buyers want to be out back where they try to get in one more final evaluation before the horse enters the sale ring. The horses are lined up at least a dozen and one-half or more deep through the barn area, in the walking ring which normally is located at the rear of the sale building and finally, in the chute leading directly into the sale ring.

On occasion, I will go to the walking ring or barn area for a final look at a prospect, but normally I will trust the evaluation our team has done and stay put. I find that if you are constantly running back and forth, it is difficult to stay focused on what you are doing, especially if your highly rated horses are closely bunched in selling order.

There are about as many approaches to bidding as there are buyers. Each person has his or her own method, but experienced buyers will vary their approach according to the situation before them. There are times, for example, when you feel someone bidding against you wants to inch the price up with the smallest increment possible. That might be the time, as long as you are staying within your price range, to increase your bid a time or two by amounts above what the auctioneer is calling for. If it is only a lukewarm bidder and you hit a couple quick, substantial raises, he will normally drop out at that point. However, if the other bidder is dead serious, he will come back with a bid to top yours and you will likely find yourself facing the go on or stop bidding decision in short order. Once again, when that happens, you must go back to your evaluation and your previously set spending limit and hold to it.

Sellers also are capable of their own misleading strategies in seeking the highest possible dollar for their yearlings. If you see a pretty yearling that the owner is really talking up as the quality of the sale, but your team has found a "hole" in conformation, pedigree or whatever, always stay with your evaluation.

Sometimes, you will be second guessing yourself when that horse comes into the ring because it seems like everybody wants it and you begin to wonder if you overlooked a valuable prospect. If the bidding is going up in dizzying fashion, it might merely mean that the owner is more aware than you about the "hole" and is trying to push the bid up quickly to create a frenzy of excitement that will end with him being rid of a problem, plus having money in his pocket. Someone new will then be confronted with the problem, minus some of their money and enthusiasm, when they discover the "hole" the yearling had when the bidding started and still has when it ended.

Anytime you are uncertain of what to do or what is happening in the bidding, be patient and wait for the auctioneer's rhythm to slow down. Once all of the frenzied bidding is over and the hype has ended, there is always that final pause on the part of the auctioneer before the hammer falls.

He may have before him the colt that was high on your list and for which someone else has just bid $40,000, the amount your team placed on him. No one else is bidding. The auctioneer will look around as he slows his chant; "forty, do I hear forty-one, forty, forty-one, forty-one anywhere?"

It may be only moments, but during that brief lull you

can decide whether to invoke your 10 percent rule and carry the horse a little higher or whether to go get a cup of coffee.

During this brief lull, if you decide to bid and the auctioneer is looking the other way and so is the bid taker, don't be shy because you aren't gong to have much time. If need be, jump right to your feet and yell, "Hey, over here!"

Better to draw some attention to yourself at this point than to get left out on a horse you really want.

And if that auctioneer looks your way a few moments later, points and says, "Sold," it will be a major thrill. If you are like most of us, your hand will be shaking when the clerk hands you the purchase agreement to sign. That brief agreement will list the horse's hip number, the amount you paid and will require your signature. Once signed, it becomes a binding agreement between you and the sale company. The check you make out for the yearling you purchase will go the sale company, which will deduct its commission and then issue its own check to the consignor.

While everyone in the Thoroughbred business has a story to tell about a great "steal" they made either at a sale or privately, the truth of the matter is that there are very few "bargains" at a horse auction. In the Thoroughbred business, the auctions are normally attended by people who are attuned to the market and who are too wise to let someone "steal" a good prospect.

When most experienced buyers get nervous is when they have evaluated a horse at, say $50,000, and bidding stops at $18,000. That's guaranteed to raise some doubts in your mind. Instead of thinking, wow, what a bargain, you are going to be wondering, what did I miss that everyone else saw?

This is where faith in the evaluation teams comes in. If you are confident that they have done their job, then stay with the game plan. By having the courage of your team's convictions, you just might have made a true bargain buy.

Of course, when dealing with a Thoroughbred yearling, you won't know for sure whether a bargain is a bargain until two years later with racing competition being the ultimate decision maker.

Several times I have mentioned the professional buyer. I don't mean to infer that because you have had far less experience, you should be intimidated by the presence of a name or reputation. They are not all geniuses. If they were, no one would have bought a million-dollar horse that couldn't run, and believe me, plenty of professional buyers have done just that. In fact, if it were possible for the professionals to be right in their evaluations and purchases all of the time, the Thoroughbred business not only wouldn't be any fun, but it would be reserved only for the wealthy who would take turns outbidding each other.

As long as there is a chance for that $7,500 yearling or the $40,000 colt you bought to one day outrun the one that some "genius" took home for $2 million, Thoroughbreds are going to continue to be a fun and satisfying sport/business.

By the way, if someone at the sale tells you what a genius he or she is, just ask one two-part question: "How many horses do you own and how many are racing?" In some cases, the answer will be, "None." I have found that it's very easy to be a genius as long as you are doing it with somebody else's money and have not put any of your own on the line. By deciding to invest money in Thoroughbred racing and going to a yearling sale to get your start, you have made a commitment that sets you above these so-called experts. Don't be overwhelmed or intimidated by them.

There is one other thing that you should be prepared for at a sale. You might still be congratulating yourself and your evaluation team on having made a good buy when someone comes rushing up and says, "Hey, I really wanted that yearling, but I missed the bidding. I'll give you an instant

$5,000 profit on it."

Here is where your rating system can come in. If the horse was on the low end of your group of prospects, take the money and bid on the next horse on your list, only this time with an additional $5,000 to spend. On the other hand, if the horse was high on your list, turn the offer down. You already have what you came for.

While having someone want to purchase your yearling at more than you paid is something of a vote of confidence in your decision, the reverse can also happen. Somebody in the "genius" category may approach you and say, "Oh, you really messed up in buying that horse, he's off in the left front," or whatever. Here again, is the time to have faith in your team and in your game plan. Stay the course.

Now that the first flush of excitement of that initial purchase has passed, don't become miserly in the next expenditures you will be called upon to make.

Every trainer can tell a story about an owner who paid $100,000 for a colt and then fired the trainer because he hired a night watchman for $50, which the owner thought was a waste of money, to keep an eye on the colt before being transported to the breaking farm the following morning.

I tell this story to make a point. If that yearling is worth $100,000 in the sale ring, it deserves the best of care and protection.

A big misconception on the part of some new owners is that racehorses take care of themselves. They don't. Let us say you were successful in buying that $40,000 yearling you have been looking for as your investment cornerstone in the Thoroughbred business. What that means is that you now have invested $40,000 in a living, breathing property. If all goes well, that property might appreciate in value and become worth $2 million.

But, because this is a living, breathing property, there

are a host of things that could go wrong and cause your property to depreciate more rapidly than anything else you could own. It's the old story of getting what you pay for at this point. If you find somebody who will board and break your horse for only a few bucks a day, you must remember that is about what you will get in return, or worse. If that horse isn't fed right, handled correctly and protected, you are going to be responsible for destroying property you invested in just as sure as the person who buys a handsome piece of real estate and then lets other people turn it into a dump.

If that pretty piece of real estate has been turned into a dump, it isn't going to fetch much on the market. If your $40,000 horse isn't properly cared for and developed, it not only isn't going to be a successful racehorse, but your entire investment is going to be in jeopardy because it is not going to be worth anything to anyone else either.

The wise investor is the one who has his plan of action formulated for the upcoming months and years, with breaking farm and trainer already designated before a hand is ever raised in the auction pavilion. If you are affiliated with a reputable trainer, all those decisions will already have been made and you will know in advance just what is going to be done with your new purchase and how much it will cost.

Now it is time to get that colt or filly off the auction grounds and into its new home where it will begin preparation for what we are hoping will be a successful and exciting racing career.

Chapter Six

The Breaking Farm

The sale is over. You are now the owner of a racehorse. You have entered a new and exciting world that will bring you into contact with a whole new group of people. Before long, you will be learning about grooms, jockeys, exercise riders, stewards, shedrows, condition books, claiming, stakes races, allowance races, photo finishes, purse money and, hopefully, the winner's circle.

What you have been through to this point has been exciting, but also stressful. The day after the sale may find you emotionally drained. After all, you have been totally caught up in this new venture, concentrating day and night just before the sale on which horses you should bid and how much, and then, finally, the nerve-wracking process of actually sitting in the pavilion and bidding on the prospects selected.

If you as a person, with powers of thought and reason, are this exhausted, think about the yearling or yearlings you have purchased who don't have that capability. Most of them are likely going to be emotional wrecks at this point. All they know is that they have been pulled from their stalls 40 times a day, looked at, led about, examined and ultimately taken into a sale ring where a lot of loud and confusing activity was taking place.

All of this has been extremely stressful to them and you can expect to find your yearling, the morning after the sale, looking pretty woebegone and exhausted. If the purchase was made at a September sale, we will have a little time to let the colt or filly recuperate, but not a whole lot if it is going to be prepared for next year's racing season as a two-year-old.

Unfortunately, the stress will continue the day immediately after the sale. The yearling has to be transported somewhere, rather than remain on the sale grounds. You, as the new owner, and your trainer will have selected the farm where the colt or filly will be broke prior to putting the youngster in training at the track.

This is a time when new owners must put their confidence in the trainer they've selected. While breaking yearlings is basically the same at all farms, your trainer will know who does it in a manner that allows him to take over without a hitch, when it's time for the youngster to move from the breaking barn to the track.

I think that a yearling needs at least five to seven days of rest and relaxation after a sale. Most of them will "hatch a bug" and become at least slightly ill in the wake of a sale. It is pretty normal for a yearling to exhibit flu-like symptoms about a week after the sale. The illness might be simply a reaction to stress or it might be from a virus picked up by being in contact with so many other yearlings. They need time to work their way through this either at a layover stable immediately after the sale or at the breaking farm.

Even when this youngster is being let down, there will be new experiences and stresses that require adjustment. Either at the layover stable or the breaking farm, the yearling will likely be turned out with others of the same age. This will require adjustment as the pecking order is established anew. In addition, your yearling is also meeting a host of new people. Gone are the familiar persons who fed and cared for it at the farm where it was raised. Instead, a new individual is at the end of the shank, leading it toward a strange van already loaded with strange horses. The ride to the breaking farm follows. That might be a long or short trip, depending on which sale the purchase was made and the farm to which the youngster is being sent. Whatever, the case, it requires still another adjustment.

At the breaking farm there will be other new people and a host of new sights and sounds to greet your prospect. On the positive side, your yearling is learning to cope with a whole new set of circumstances and likely is gaining confidence in the process.

After a week or two of adjustment, your yearling is ready to set out on the long road toward the winner's circle. There are just as many unknowns at this point as there were when you raised that last bid. Is your yearling going to be coming out of the starting gate at Churchill Downs the first Saturday in May of its three-year-old year, or is it going to be entered at some track in the first race of the day for a $15,000 claiming tag? There are no crystal balls to provide the answer. Only training and time will do that.

From the moment the yearling arrives at the breaking farm, data will be begin to be collected which will keep you informed as to just how well your prospect is doing. Developing a successful racehorse is a step by step process, much like constructing a building. Getting the horse properly broke lays the foundation and provides our first indicators of whether the prospect truly possesses the four necessary traits that I mentioned earlier - mental toughness, soundness, ability and a strong/healthy immune system.

At this point, you as the new owner, will also begin getting better acquainted with the people you've decided on to help you in your quest for a winner - your trainer and his staff and, through the trainer, the staff at the breaking farm.

If you find you aren't in synch mentally with the people with whom you are affiliated, you must make changes.

However, if you find that early on in your experience as

a new owner, you are making those changes with some frequency, it might be time to take a good, long look inward. Nobody is right all of the time and nobody is wrong all of the time. It just might be that the problem lies with you rather than the people with whom you're affiliated.

The thing I can't emphasize enough to new owners at this point is that trainers aren't miracle workers. They cannot make a horse run faster than it is physically able, even if the owner has paid a million dollars for it. The trainer's job is to get that horse to perform to the maximum of its ability and to keep it sound in the process. There are no real shortcuts and miracles are pretty scarce in the Thoroughbred business.

The trainer's role is akin to that of a coach. His job is to spot the strengths and weaknesses of his players and then come up with a training strategy to maximize the strengths and nullify or at least minimize the weaknesses.

Each horse will differ in physical and mental ability. It is for that reason that it's difficult to set forth a routine training program that is the same for each horse. Sometimes the problems a trainer faces are mental and sometimes they are physical. He has to know the difference.

A gelding named Rut that I had in training is an example of a physical problem preventing the horse from performing to its maximum. In this case, the root of the problem was physical, but what it caused the horse to do was a mental reaction. When this horse came into training, he appeared to have ability, but it was being compromised by the fact that whenever he came to a shadow on the track, he'd jump it.

Jockey Jerry Bailey rode Rut in a race at Gulfstream where he jumped a shadow. Bailey said it appeared as though the horse didn't see the shadow until he was right upon it, which startled him and caused the leap. We decided we better have an ophthalmologist take a look at Rut's eyes in case something was wrong physically.   Dr. Lorraine Karpinski conducted the examination and found that there was a lesion in the left eye which, simply put, meant that he had a blind spot. Technically, it was called a retinal scar ventral. Because of the blind spot, he couldn't detect a shadow on the track as he approached, but it would become visible just as he got to it and this startled him and caused him to jump.

There was no treatment for the eye, so we had to come up with a way to nullify the problem with equipment. The answer was a special Australian blinker called a Pelling Passifier. Both eyes are covered with a screen, of which the bottom half is covered with black tape which prevents him from seeing shadows on the ground.

Rut's vision problem made him more dependent on his hearing to tell him what was going on around him and this, too, was part of his problem. He would shy away from noise in the grandstand. We solved this by running him in earmuffs, similar to the ones Gate Dancer wore.

While we couldn't solve the physical problem as there was no cure for it, we could nullify it and, in the process, solve what had become a mental problem as well. As this is being written, Rut is in the midst of a successful career at the allowance race level.

The ability to solve those types of problems while bringing the prospect to its peak of potential is the trainer's job and, basically, the process begins the moment the yearling steps off the van at the breaking farm. It is for this reason that the farm selected has to be one with which the trainer is familiar so that the first building blocks are set into place through communication between the breaking farm and the trainer.

This brings us to a basic question.

What should training involve?

There   are   a   thousand   variables   in   training

Thoroughbreds. An approach that is correct for one horse, might be totally wrong for another. The trainer must look at that horse as an individual and then take whatever steps are necessary to provide for that particular horse's needs.

In training, the only absolute is the fact that there are no absolutes.

There are those who will argue that we train our Thoroughbreds at too early an age. I disagree. I strongly believe that, after being broke as long yearlings - 18 months to 2 years of age - Thoroughbreds should be trained on the track as two-year-olds.

It has been argued that two-year-olds suffer more injuries than any other age group of Thoroughbreds. That may be true, but one of the reasons for that is that serious training brings out all of the horse's structural weaknesses. There are going to be fewer injuries by age group after the two-year-old year because a number with structural weaknesses already have been weeded out.

If we waited until these youngsters were three years old, I firmly believe that the injury rate would be even higher. Obviously, I am not talking about spending a couple weeks with a two-year-old on the track and then declaring him fit and ready to start. I am talking about developing a colt or filly in a slow, easy manner beginning at two years of age and continuing on through its racing career with a common-sense program.

Unless exercised and worked, a horse is not going to stimulate the development of strong, dense bones, tough, resilient ligaments and tendons, nor the muscles needed for support and to propel its body along at speed. If you wait until a colt or filly is three years of age before beginning this exercise and training regimen, you will wind up dealing with a much heavier body that must be supported by undeveloped bones, ligaments, tendons and muscles. The chances of that structure being injured in training increase.

Back to the breaking farm. As an owner, you should know that there are a number of ways to get a young Thoroughbred started. The successful methods are designed to get the horse familiar with weight on its back, being steered with bridle and bit and traveling in the company of others. The good breaking farms take their time and move on to step two, only after step one has been successfully implemented, and so on.

It will likely be at least a month at the breaking farm before anyone actually· gets on your new purchase's back. Early on, the staff will be teaching the youngster to respond to the bit. At some farms, they will accomplish this with a special bitting rig which is a light harness that enables the trainer to drive the colt or filly in long lines from the ground, teaching it to go left when we pull on the left line and vice versa to the right.

They might also do some of the preliminary conditioning by ponying your yearling. This involves leading the youngster while riding another horse that is calm and unflappable.

After about 30 days at the breaking farm, your yearling is ready to feel the weight of a human on its back for the first time. This a traumatic time for a youngster because the flight or fight mechanism mentioned earlier kicks in again. It is unnatural for a horse to have weight on its back. In the horse's early years, if it felt weight on its back, it meant one thing - a predator had leaped down upon it and was in a position to deal a death blow with claws or fangs.

That ingrained fear has not been bred out of modern-day horses so we have to get them used to having weight on their back gradually and do it in a way that nullifies the inherent fear. Again, as with so many things involved in training, horses will differ in their acceptance of weight on their back. Some seem scarcely to notice while others will never completely get over the jitters when a rider first mounts up and, without needing an excuse, might seek to dislodge the rider.

Generally, the first step in getting a horse to accept a rider is taken where the horse feels the most safe - in its stall. It will usually start with someone just half laying over the horse's back while a helper maintains control over the horse with a lead shank attached to the halter. Later, the rider will get astride, often without a saddle, and just sit there quietly while the horse is led about in its stall. Again, progress will be on an individual basis. One horse might calmly accept a rider on its back after only a day or two. With another, it might take up to 10 days of what is actually desensitizing before the horse is ready to permit someone to be on its back and remain there.

As each step is accomplished quietly and safely, another is taken. The saddle is introduced and before long the yearling is being ridden about in a small paddock or up and down an alleyway.

At this point, the youngster is not being shown a race track. Instead, exercise under saddle often comes in the form of group trail rides across grassy fields and through trees. There is a lot of walking and jogging as they slowly, but steadily take this soft yearling and develop its bones, muscles and suspensory system to withstand the upcoming rigors of training and racing.

(Technically, the yearling remains a yearling through December 31 of the year following birth. January 1 is the universal birthday for all horses, no matter when during the year they were born. In other words, every yearling becomes a two-year-old on a given January 1st even though, chronologically, they may only be 22 or 23 months of age, or even less).

While the bodies of these youngsters are being developed at the breaking farm, so are their minds. Again, we come back to the matter of training young horses as two-year-olds rather than as three-year-olds. Not only does the two-year-old have a lighter body as far as bulk is concerned, plus more elasticity of bones and sinews, but its mind is also more open and receptive.

By the time a horse is three years of age, it's already getting at least somewhat set in its ways and that can mean that it will find more ways to hurt itself in resisting breaking and training efforts.

As the yearlings at the breaking farm are being ridden regularly, the first signs concerning mental traits will emerge. As the training continues, the yearlings will be ridden in groups, also referred to as sets. How they react to this activity, may be an indicator of how they will react when in formal training and racing. Hopefully, your new purchase will be both calm and bold. Our desire is that it be a horse that always wants to be in front, but yet is calm enough that it doesn't dance around nervously, wasting energy, in an effort to get there.

From walking and jogging, the youngsters at the breaking farm will graduate to galloping. As they become more fit physically the distances galloped will be increased as will the speed. By the time they leave the breaking farm and come to me, I like to see them doing a half mile in around 55 or 56 seconds. If they have reached that point at the breaking farm, it tells me that these young horses have the kind of muscle tone, skeletal and suspensory development that will enable them to go on with more serious race training on the track.

The breaking farm will also be varying the sets or groups that your yearling is in. They will be trying to find out how it reacts when in the company of the varying personalities of other horses in training. How does your colt or filly react when paired with a strong-willed, go forward horse, for example? What happens when it's traveling beside one that is nervous and skittish? Our clues as to mental traits are continuing to surface at this point.

By now, some of the other traits are also beginning to be manifested. Hopefully all of the following questions elicit a positive response.

Is your yearling staying sound? Is its immune system keeping it healthy? Is it demonstrating that first inkling of ability by moving along at the gallop effortlessly with an efficient, ground-covering stride? Are its hooves holding up? Is it utilizing its feed ration properly, as evidenced by a sleek, glossy coat?

At this point, we don't want your young prospect to look like a fat show horse. Fat will slow it down instead of speed it up. If you go to see your yearling at the breaking farm and find yourself looking at a bright-eyed, calm, confident individual that loves to go out and be exercised; with just a ripple of ribs showing beneath a sleek coat, you can be confident that nothing has occurred to this point to lower the expectations you had during that exhilarating moment in the sale ring when the auctioneer looked your way and said, "Sold."

If, however, your yearling looks like it's ready to be shown in hand at a horse show, it means that the youngster's body has not been properly prepared for further training or racing.

A racehorse must be a lean machine to perform at its maximum and stay sound. The fit racehorse never loses its conditioning nor its glossy coat.

One of the final things a breaking farm may do is get your youngster familiar with the starting gate. When they come to me as two-year-olds, I like to have them at least familiar enough with the starting gate that they will walk through it calmly.

By now, several months have passed and the new year

has been ushered in. The prospect you purchased as a yearling is now officially a two-year-old. You and the trainer have been apprised by the breaking farm staff of their evaluation of your prospect. They have done everything they can to get your youngster fit mentally and physically for what lies ahead.

The race track.

Chapter Seven

Learning at the Track

When a two-year-old comes to the track from a breaking farm, it's another time of stress. There are new people to get used to, new sights, sounds and above all, a new routine.

Comparatively speaking, your young prospect has lived a pretty casual life on the farm. It was fed in the morning, ridden, bathed and then perhaps turned out in a paddock where it could wander about at leisure and relax. About mid afternoon, it was returned to its stall and a bit later, it was fed its evening meal. The next morning, the routine started all over again.

Just being outdoors in a paddock can have a relaxing and sometimes tiring effect on a horse when compared to the more structured existence at the track. Reducing it to human terms, it's a bit like the difference between staying at home in your air-conditioned house on a warm summer day and going on a camping trip.

If you're outside all day and the wind is blowing and you're hiking about and using energy, you're going to be ready to hit the bed that night after a hot, relaxing shower. The next day you're feeling fine again, but maybe without quite the same energy you had the previous day because you're still a little tired physically.

If you'd stayed at home in your air-conditioned house, you wouldn't feel that tired physically, but you might be tired mentally if you were working on some project that occupied your mind.

At the breaking farm, your young prospect, because of the routine along with the outdoor paddock exercise, was probably more tired physically than mentally. At the track it will be the reverse. Here, the horse is in a stall for all but about an hour or so each day. It will have all the water and food it requires and will be asked to work only for a brief time each day. Thus, it will rarely get exhausted physically, but as the training pressure increases, so does the mental pressure.

It is here that one of the four necessary traits for success comes into full play - mental toughness.

In training your two-year-old when it arrives at the track, we aren't, figuratively speaking, going to just toss it into the water to learn whether it will sink or swim. Instead, we're going to ease it into its new environment and let it adjust

Hand walking the young horse around the shedrow helps it relax in its new surroundings.

Photo by Les Sellnow

gradually to the new regimen.

During the first two or three days that young horses are in my shedrow, I'll just have them hand walked so they can become familiar with their surroundings. This means that a groom or hot walker will simply lead the youngster around the walking path that circles the barn. The horse will have on a halter and lead shank which will be in the hands of a calm, experienced person.

When the youngsters relax during the hand walking, it's time to move on to another step. Now your two-year-old is saddled and bridled, just like at the breaking farm and an exercise rider climbs aboard. However, we don't head right for the track at this point. We want to make certain that the colt or filly has accepted its new surroundings in a quiet and

The exercise rider rides the youngster at a walk through the shedrow to make certain the horse has accepted its new surroundings before heading to the track.
Photo by Les Sellnow

relaxed enough manner so as not to be a danger to itself or

anyone else. To achieve this, I'll just have the exercise rider ride around the shedrow at a walk.

Once again, the key for moving on will be a relaxed attitude. When the horse is traveling around the shedrow quietly and taking in all the sights and sounds calmly, but with a curious attitude, it's time to head for the race track.

Riding the youngsters through the backside in the company of an older, experienced horse helps the young horses relax in their new surroundings.
Photo by Les Sellnow

While the horse is being hand walked and ridden in the shedrow, I'm studying it, attempting to learn its personality; trying to get to know it intimately so I will know how to adjust to its needs during training. This isn't a time to put a young horse into a pre-planned regimen and carry it through whether the horse is happy or not. This is the period when a horse should be given every opportunity to get to know and trust the new people handling it, adjust to what might be a change in diet and feeding regimen, and above all, become comfortable in what is a whole new atmosphere. The horse will have to make adjustments, that's for certain, but the most important thing is for the training staff to adjust to the needs of the horse.

This is the trainer's first opportunity to really get to know the young prospect and he or she should make the most of it. You can get a good feel for a horse's personality just by observing how it adjusts to shedrow life if you take the time to observe.

Is the horse overly aggressive? Does it reach over its stall webbing and snap at other horses going by? Does it get nervous and anxious when there are unusual noises? Is it frightened by sudden movement when being walked around the shedrow? Does it enjoy being groomed, or does it become anxious? Does it clean up its food each day, or does it pace about the stall nervously at feeding time, grabbing only a mouthful of grain as it passes the feed box?

I mentioned earlier that anybody can train a racehorse if you know horses. Well, the only way to get to know horses is to observe them closely. It is the trainer's job to, figuratively at least, crawl inside that horse's mind and look out.

Only then can you figure out why a horse reacts as it does in certain circumstances. Once you truly understand what the horse is doing and why, you can take the next step which involves nullifying whatever it is that produces harmful stress and, on a more positive note, maximize that which seems to produce a beneficial effect.

Hopefully, your $40,000 prospect is a calm, confident young horse that likes people and takes change in stride. When led from the stall on the shedrow, it walks along willingly, ears pricked forward to pick up all the new sounds while its eyes are quietly recording all the activity swirling about it. When the exercise rider climbs aboard for the first time, it walks forward with long, confident strides, enjoying the opportunity to stretch its muscles.

83

If that's the case, it will be only a matter of a few days before we take this two-year-old to the track.

This is a tense time. Even though your colt or filly might be calm and relaxed in the shedrow, going to the track the first time can be traumatic. It may have been exercised on a track at the breaking farm, but that will have been done on a smaller oval and with far fewer horses around.

If the youngster has come to the track with another prospect and the two have been in the same set (the group or couples that train together) at the breaking farm, I normally will leave them together when we first start taking them to the track. In addition, because the sights and sounds of a training

Sights and sounds of early morning training hours can make the track a scary place for a young horse.
Photo by Les Sellnow

track in the morning can produce anxiety in the calmest of youngsters, we'll likely send along a veteran horse that is familiar with all that's going on and is undisturbed by it. This might be a veteran racehorse or it might be a quiet track pony that will calm the youngsters, simply by walking along quietly and nonchalantly.

The track during training hours is a pretty scary place for a young horse. Some horses out there are traveling around at speed while some are jogging in the opposite direction. There are the sounds of people yelling back and forth along with nonstop conversation between trainers, exercise riders and track help.

That is a lot of commotion for a young horse to absorb and adjust to. If it is in the company of a calm stablemate, or racetrack veteran, however, it normally will make the adjustment very quickly and, if it has the mental traits we have been hoping for, it will look forward to its morning trips to the track with eagerness once the adjustment has been made.

Mental traits. It is at this point in the horse's development that we will be concentrating on that ingredient with the most intensity. It is still too early to determine whether the colt or filly has ability. It should be remaining sound because little physical stress has been placed on it. (Generally, any unsoundness that shows up at this point is the result of an accident.) Once the young prospect has picked up and conquered the routine viruses that afflict about 99 percent of the two-year-olds coming to the track, its immune system should be functioning well. So, two of the traits, soundness and a good immune system, are in place. Ability is an unknown quantity and mental toughness is beginning to come into focus.

While we have been able to get a feel for the young prospect in the shedrow, it is at the track that its mental traits will truly be revealed and it is now that we will study them with intensity. Hopefully, your $40,000 prospect will display both calmness and boldness when going to the track in the early stages. We want him or her to march right into that flurry of activity with a calm, but curious approach, just the

Riding the young horse to the gap allows it to take in all the on-track activity.

Photo by Les Sellnow

way it adjusted to its new life on the shedrow.

If, on the other hand, we have a horse that gets nervous and does not want to go onto the track, we have to seek ways to nullify that stress. Maybe it will involve ponying the nervous horse for a few days from the back of a quiet stable pony, or maybe it will involve riding the horse to the gap - the opening onto the track - and just having the exercise rider sit there quietly so the nervous youngster can take in all the sights and sounds without entering into the mainstream of on-track activity until it relaxes.

Whatever it takes, the nervous horse must be helped so that it learns to cope with the on-track stress or a successful future will be in doubt. Nervousness on race day can burn up tons of energy that would be better used for racing speed and staying power.

We will continue to watch these young prospects closely

as they graduate to the point where they are galloping around the track. At this point, we will also start looking for that important trait called ability. How easily does that colt or filly gallop? Are they relaxed when galloping? Do they travel with balance and rhythm instead of legs flying every which way? After they've galloped a mile are they still relaxed or are they fretful and stressed when pulled up?

Ponying the two-year-old from the back of a quiet stable pony can help the horse with on-track stress.

Photo by Les Sellnow

After about 10 days, I like to get a light breeze in on these youngsters. When we breeze a horse, we increase the speed beyond the stage of galloping. With the two-year-olds that are new to the track, I will have the exercise riders breeze them a half mile in 55 to 56 seconds, about what has already been asked of them at the breaking farm.

You accomplish a couple things with this early breeze. First, you let the youngsters get the feel of running on a big track. Generally speaking, the track at the breaking farm will have been smaller and with less activity. You also get another hint as to ability as you watch how the horse travels when asked for more speed. And, of course, you get even more information on the mental traits.

Did it relish that burst of speed or did it become agitated and nervous? Obviously, we want to be training a horse that loves to run, but does so in controllable fashion. We do not want one that charges off with wild abandon. Nor do we want to see it becoming stressed when speed is called for, causing it to deplete its energy bank because of nervousness.

The reason the horse is at the track in the first place is to run and I want to give them an opportunity to do just that as soon as they appear to be relaxed and ready, thus the early breeze.

Next comes the starting gate and once again we will get more clues on the horse's mental traits. The youngster will likely have been exposed to the starting gate on the breaking farm, but we want to go back to the basics to make certain that the starting gate is a pleasant experience and will be approached with confidence by our two-year-old.

At the track, there will be either one or two starting gates for schooling the young horses. One will generally be located in the long chute leading into the backstretch where races under one mile are started. This is the one we will use for the young prospect. In the beginning, the exercise rider will simply ride the youngster in from the rear of the gate and then out through the front just as was done on the breaking farm.

The goal is to get the young horse relaxed in the gate, but yet ready to run. There are two basic reasons that the young horse must learn to handle the starting gate well.

The first is that official gate approval is needed before it will ever be permitted to start a race. The second is that good manners and an attentive attitude in the gate will give our horse that little extra edge at the start when the gate springs open during a race.

So, shortly after arrival at the track, it is back to the basics at the gate. When the colt or filly has walked through to our satisfaction, realizing anew that this big green monster isn't going to harm them, it's time for them to be closed up inside the gate. This can be a time of anxiety and trauma for the young horse. A gate crew employed by the track will be there to work with the exercise rider and trainer. Their calmness and patience are a must at this point.

They will be told by the trainer that this two-year-old has been walked through a gate, but has never been closed up in one. One of the gate crew will, first of all, lead the horse into the gate from the rear and then on out the front. If the horse shows no signs of stress or anxiety, the attendant will then lead the horse into the gate and bring it to a halt.

Once inside, a second attendant will close the rear gate. The person leading the horse now will be at the front gate and will quietly close it. A lot of young horses will feel trapped and become nervous and agitated as the front and rear gate barriers close on them. It is time for the exercise rider and the gate crew to remain very calm, insisting that the young horse remain in the gate, but petting and talking in soothing tones to allay its fears.

When the horse relaxes, the front gate is opened very slowly and quietly and the rider will walk the horse out. Later as the horse relaxes and becomes more confident between the front and rear gate barriers, we will ask the attendants to close the front gate before we ever walk the horse in. Just when the two-year-old is ready for this depends on temperament. If the horse is quiet and confident, we usually will be able to walk it into a gate with the front closed at about the third session.

At this point the horse is going to have another new experience. When it enters the gate with the front closed and the rear barrier then is closed, it's time for the assistant starter to step up on the rail beside the horse's head, just like he will do on race day. That is quite an experience for a young horse. Remember, the assistant starter is on the ground and he has to

With both front and rear barriers closed, the assistant starter steps up next to the horse's head. The exercise rider and the assistant starter work to reassure the horse. Before long, the horse accepts the gate and is ready to start moving out when the front is opened.
Photo by Les Sellnow

get up on the railing very close to the horse's head and neck. When the assistant starter, calm and careful though he might be, climbs up beside that colt or filly's head the first time, it often frightens the horse. The assistant starter will pet the horse and talk to it and before long, the youngster will be accepting the man's presence without being concerned.

When the front of the gate is opened at this point, it is done in a quiet manner and, as the sessions continue, the horse graduates from walking out to trotting out and, finally, to galloping out.

I have found it best to do gate training in company; two or three of these babies at one time. If one of them happens to be calm and relaxed, we will pair it with one that is skittish. The calm one will have a soothing influence on the other and we will take them into the gate at the same time. Of course, if you pair up two young horses that are skittish and afraid of the gate, they will just learn to mess up even more instead of settling down. If two of the youngsters are skittish, it is time to break them up as a set and pair them with a quiet, older horse.

If the horse is totally relaxed in the gate, we may take it there only two or three times a week. If it is nervous and concerned, we may take it to the gate every day; just walking it in, letting it stand there and then backing it out. At this point we want our young prospect to be totally relaxed in the gate.

I like to let young horses gallop out of the starting gate early on in their training. After about the fourth or fifth time out of the gate and I see that they're handling it in a calm, relaxed manner, I will just have the exercise rider let them gallop out of the gate, remain at the gallop until they reach the half-mile pole and then stride breeze them on to the wire. A stride breeze is traveling the half mile in about 53 to 54 seconds.

By letting the horse finish the half mile in a stride breeze, we are letting it know that it can and should run after coming out of the gate. Yet, we are not putting any pressure on the youngster for speed, so the horse should be remaining calm and relaxed.

Along about the fourth or fifth week of training, I will have these youngsters breezing a bit faster. By now they will be doing a half mile at a 51 to 52-second clip or better and they are ready to gallop stronger out of the starting gate.

If they are handling all this very well, it is time to begin simulating race day conditions. We will take three or four two-year-olds to the starting gate and the attendants will lead them in. Now, for the first time in their lives these young horses will hear the bell ring that signals the start of the race and the gates will fly open as the starter pushes the button that rings a bell and electronically allows the gates to spring open with a bang.

We won't be expecting your young prospect to break sharply the first time out of the gate. Normally, it's going to take three or four starts with the bell before the horse leaves the gate quickly, running hard from the first jump.

No horse is permitted to start in a race until it proves that it can stand quietly with the gate closed and leave running when it opens. Normally the gate approval will come at the second or third trip. At that point the assistant starter will sign a card to be presented to the track steward stating that the horse has received its starting gate approval. The steward will also sign the card and then it will be filed in the racing secretary's office.

Just what kind of works the young prospect is getting at this stage of training depends on the horse. Generally speaking, works, which means the horse is allowed to run at speed for a predetermined distance such as a half mile or five-eighths of a mile, are conducted as the horse tells you. How far and how fast each youngster is worked will depend on the way in which it is developing.

There's the old adage in boxing that you don't want to leave your fight in the training ring. The same is true of racing. You don't want to leave your race on the training track. You want the horse to go into a race sharply tuned and bursting with energy, not listless because it ran so hard in training sessions that there wasn't anything left on race day.

By the time the two-year-old gets its starting card, if everything has gone along without a hitch, we are into the on-track training program by eight to 10 weeks and are somewhere between one to three weeks from giving this colt or filly its first start in a race.

Somewhere along the way during the early part of training, however, nature often throws the young horse a curve in the form of bucked shins. With some colts and fillies the soreness from bucked shins will be severe enough to force a stoppage of training, while with others, it's only a discomfort and they can train through it, though they may not be able to gallop or breeze for a couple weeks.

Bucked shins, generally speaking, are an inflammation of the periosteum which is the membrane that covers the cannon bones. As training progresses, the stress of galloping and breezing on that relatively long and fragile bone causes it to undergo dramatic changes as the body rushes in to strengthen it to meet the new demands being placed upon it. Sometimes the stresses even cause micro fractures along the surface of the bone which must be repaired by the body with a new layer of calcium. While all these structural changes are going on, painful inflammation of the periosteum is often an unwanted result. We know the bone is being strengthened, but the soreness that often accompanies it, forces us to change training tactics.

In severe cases, the young horse may be sent back to its home farm for a month or two of rest and recuperation. In other cases, the treatment consists of backing off on the training regimen until the inflammation departs. It might be necessary to just ride these lightly afflicted horses at a walk in the shedrow for five or six days and then begin jogging them on the track. However, you normally would not do any breezing for two weeks, even in mild cases.

Once the inflammation is gone, it's a sign that the body has repaired the damage and the youngster is ready to resume a more serious training schedule.

If a youngster needs additional time off to recuperate and is sent home, no one should lose sight of the fact that we're still building a fit racehorse even though serious training has been suspended for the moment. What I mean by this is, I do not want to see that horse come back to the track a month or so later weighing a hundred pounds more than when it left.

Again, we can use a human comparison. Let's assume you are used to running and are conditioned to do it. Then something happens that requires you to undergo surgery or whatever and this requires a cessation of your running. Now, if you gain 50 pounds while recovering from your surgery, you are going to be in mighty poor condition to resume what had been your normal running routine. Not only did your muscles get softer while you were recovering, but now you are carrying extra weight. It doesn't take much imagination to realize that before you can get into good shape again and run with the same energy and ability as before the surgery, you are going to have to shed some pounds.

So it is with the horse that gets turned out for rest and recuperation and gains unneeded and unwanted weight. Instead of making a fast comeback, its progress will be slow.

Once through the bucked shin problem and back in serious training, it is time to take an overall serious look at our $40,000 prospect.

Let's assume the youngster is cleaning up its food with relish at each feeding. (One of the basic signals that a horse isn't feeling well or is suffering from too much harmful stress is when it doesn't clean up a ration that it normally devours. Conversely, you must also make certain that the horse that will eat everything in sight is converting that food to lean, hard muscles and not soft fat.) Its mind is healthy. It is eager for each morning's workout. It stands quietly in the starting gate, but is ready to burst forth alertly when the gate opens, moving at speed, but still remaining calm and relaxed. It covers the ground with a long, fluid stride and is now doing a half mile in 49 or 50 seconds with ease.

All four essential traits seem to be in place at the moment. The youngster is sound. It's good immune system has it healthy and with a robust appetite. It is mentally tough and happy. It travels with an easy, ground covering stride that bespeaks ability.

On the other hand, we may have another youngster that one time out will breeze along calmly and confidently and another time will just seem to lose it. Sometimes it cleans up its food and sometimes it doesn't. Sometimes when watching it gallop, we get the feeling that it just hasn't grown into its body yet. It lacks coordination and smoothness of stride.

One of these young horses is ready to go to the races and one isn't. One is going to need more time to develop and the other is ready to take on all comers.

Hopefully, the call you, as the new owner receives from the trainer is an encouraging one concerning the young prospect you bought at the sale for $40,000. If the gist of the message is that your two-year-old is ready for its first official test on the track, you're ready for an exhilarating experience. You may have thought you experienced excitement at the sale when you were the successful bidder. Well, the tension and excitement of race day is going to surpass that.

Chapter Eight

Responsibilities of Ownership

While the prime responsibility for getting a horse ready for its first start rests with the trainer, there are a couple things for which the owner is responsible. First and foremost, he or she must become licensed by the racing jurisdiction where the horse is going to run. This means filling out a routine form asking the name of the trainer handling your horse and some basic information about the horses you have in training. The form is supplied by a state's racing commission and, after being filled out, is submitted to it along with a licensing fee.

Only licensed owners are permitted to enter horses in races.

The other responsibility is a bit more exciting. The owner must decide on the colors for his or her silks as well as the design. There are commercial firms that make the silks to order. In essence, silks become the owner's shield or coat of arms; his or her identity on the track. Personally, I like to see owners select lighter colors because they are easier to pick up visually as the horse goes around the track.

When properly licensed, colors selected and filed with the racing commission and the silks transported to the jockeys' quarters at the track, it's time to get ready for race-day excitement.

First, however, there are a few more basic details to attend to with our two-year-old. One of them is identification.

Every Thoroughbred that races must be identified with a written record of its name, color and markings and also with a tattoo on its upper lip. A person employed by the racing commission will come by the barn and examine the horse from top to bottom, noting the horse's name, all markings, color, white hairs, and any unique patterns or swirls in hair growth. The horse will also be assigned an identification number which will be tattooed into the upper lip. This information is filed with the Jockey Club.

The tattooed number remains with the horse for life and is checked by an identifier each and every time it races to make certain that the horse is the one listed by the trainer at the entry box.

It's now time to pick the race where our young prospect will receive its baptism by fire. Generally, we'll be looking for a race of only about five furlongs in length. A furlong is one-eighth of a mile so we're looking at a race that will be no longer than the two-year-old already is breezing.

Most tracks will start their two-year-old races at four and one-half furlongs in the spring - about late April - and then will extend the distances as spring moves into summer. By June, they'll be offering six-furlong races for two-year-olds in most jurisdictions.

Your young prospect is going to be entered in a four and one-half furlong race for maidens, which means young horses who either have never started a race or, if they've started, haven't won.

Hopefully, we have found a race for the young prospect about 10 days after receiving gate approval. Once we've found the right race, it's time for making additional contacts to get everything in readiness. One of the most important elements is the jockey who will guide the youngster on its maiden voyage. When the horse goes to the starting gate for its approval ticket, I like to have the jockey aboard who will be aboard in its first race. I'll want to get a good work in on the youngster that day, and it will be to everyone's advantage if the jockey is the one doing the riding.

Now that the two-year-old is properly identified and has its gate approval, there still is something about which it knows nothing at this point. That is the paddock where it will be saddled prior to the race. At this point the young colt or filly has never seen a paddock, has never experienced a crowd of people and has never taken the long walk from the backside to the grandstand in the afternoon.

If we want this young prospect to perform at its best the first time out, we'll want to give it some experience in a paddock prior to the first race. Accommodations for paddock schooling can be made through the paddock judge, the individual in charge of that phase of activity on race day.

We'll ask what day and during which race it would be most convenient to have the youngster brought over. Once that's been established, we'll lead the two-year-old to the saddling paddock just like we will do on race day. We will stand it in a paddock stall so it can see and hear all of the activity and learn that no harm is going to be directed its way. The youngster's groom will be there as will the trainer, so the young horse will have familiar people on which to focus for calming support.

We may decide to go ahead and saddle the young colt or filly in the paddock and perhaps use this as the first opportunity to acquaint it with an over-girth. To understand the over-girth, we must explain the difference between the training saddle to which the two-year-old has become familiar and the jockey's saddle it will wear when racing.

The training saddle is larger than the jockey's saddle, so that's a basic difference. However, the most significant difference has to do with the girths. The training saddle has a girth that buckles into place, leather on leather, on the right side and then is cinched up on the left side. The leather of the girth on this side gives way to a section of elastic material which provides some flex when tightening the girth. With the jockey's saddle, there are two girths and both of them are of elastic material. The reason for this is that the elastic will expand and retract as the horse breathes deeply during a race.

First, the saddle is cinched into place with the under-girth and then the over-girth goes on over the entire saddle to lock it into place. Having two elasticized girths pulled tight around its middle can be traumatic for a young horse the first time it's done. With most young horses, however, it won't be cause for serious concern.

Once the paddock schooling is over and all else is in readiness, it's time to get the youngster entered in the race. To do this, the trainer will go to the racing secretary's office on the grounds at least 48 hours before race time to make the entry.

When entering, we'll give the horse's name (it must be on file), the owner's name (he or she must be licensed), the colors (they must be on file), the jockey's name, the weight being carried, any approved medication that will be used on race day, along with the horse's sex and age.

Next comes the drawing for post position, which happens after entries close, in the secretary's office. Let's assume that your two-year-old is one of 12 entered for a particular race. Twelve "pills", each containing a number from 1 to 12, are placed in a plastic container, shaped much like a soda bottle. The bottle is shaken up and a number is taken out. At the same time the entry sheets from the horses entered have been shuffled about in their box and one of them is drawn at the same time as the number.

If the number from the pill bottle is three and the entry sheet drawn out at the same time is for a horse we'll call Speedy Demon, then Speedy Demon has post position number three. The process continues until all 12 pills have been matched with an entry sheet.

In case there are more than 12 entries and 12 was the maximum field permitted for the race - let's say there were 16 horses entered for the race in question - the horses not drawn go on an "also eligible" list. If one of the 12 scratches, then one of the eligible four is drawn to replace it. A scratch time will be listed by the track and, under normal circumstances, you will scratch, if you so decide to do so, within that framework of time. If, however, the horse is injured in an accident or becomes lame, it can be scratched right up to post time.

Now all the paperwork is completed - the youngster is entered in the first race of its career and, of course, we all know that this is the greatest horse to ever set foot on a track.

On the morning of race day, everyone will get to the barn in the early hours as usual. Because we know that the young prospect not only is going to race that day, but is going to be in one of the early races on the card, it is going to be one of the first to be trained.

The training that morning will take one of three forms - riding at a walk around the shedrow, jogging a mile on the track, or galloping a mile. If the horse is a strong two-year-old and well advanced in training, I might opt for the mile gallop.

By the time the young prospect gets back to the barn, the groom has cleaned and prepared its stall and is ready to give it a bath. That finished, the horse is put back into the stall. Now, however, instead of putting up the hay net as we normally would so the horse can eat its fill, we'll just give it a flake of hay. We'll give it plenty of fresh water but won't offer grain until about 9 or 10 a.m. At that time, we'll give it half a ration of grain. I don't want a lot of food in there come race time.

If the horse goes to eating the straw in its stall, we'll put on a muzzle. A veteran horse will know at this point that it's race day and they will just kind of settle into a comfortable spot in their stall and relax, almost as though they are focusing on what they're going to be asked to do a little later. The young prospect won't know exactly what is going on, but it only takes a race or two before they, too, will find a spot in their stall where they feel comfortable to await the trip to the saddling paddock.

At about 12:14 to 12:30 p.m., if the colt or filly is in the 1:30 race, the barn foreman or assistant trainer will come to the stall after the horse is cleaned up and before the bridle is put on, to put bandages on the rear legs. These are commercial bandages that run down the rear leg, starting well below the hock and covering the fetlock joint. They are an elasticized bandage and the prime purpose they serve is to protect the sesamoid bones located at the rear of the fetlock. These bandages are known as run downs.

Some trainers also will put running bandages on the front legs. I don't do this unless the horse is in a claiming race. (More about that in another chapter.)

Now with the bandages on the rear legs, the groom takes over, brushing the horse's coat and combing out the mane and tail. Sometimes grooms will braid the mane on the morning of race day; when they comb it out early in the afternoon, it fluffs out beautifully.

If the track is muddy, some trainers will tie up the horse's tail so it doesn't collect mud. I do not do this because I feel the tail is used by the horse as a balancing mechanism and I want it to be flowing free and natural. I leave the tail alone.

The race bridle goes on and after it's in place, we put on a tongue tie. Before tying the tongue, we'll rinse the mouth out with water to make certain there are no food particles or debris that might be sucked into the lungs during the race. The tongue tie is a strip of cloth about two inches wide that goes over the tongue and is tied in place beneath the jaw. I like to affix the tongue tie in the stall rather than in the paddock

102

because the horse is more relaxed at the barn. The tongue tie is not a painful device. Its purpose is to prevent the horse from getting its tongue over the bit. If the tongue gets balled up at the rear of the mouth, it can hinder breathing.

Our method of tying the tongue allows the horse to do just about anything it normally would with its tongue except get it over the bit. We throw a half-hitch around the tongue and then tie a square knot. I guarantee that if done this way, the tongue tie will not hurt the horse, but I also guarantee that it won't come undone, even though it is not pulled tight nor twisted.

Post position numbers are given out as the horses make their way from the backside to the saddling paddock.
Photo by Les Sellnow

It's time to head for the paddock. This will mark the second time this youngster has made that walk. But, this time it's different and I swear, even these young horses sense that it's different. They know this isn't going to be just a schooling session. They don't know what to expect. They just know there is a different feeling in the air.

s the horse is led onto the track, the first official it will encounter is the person in charge of numbers. He or she will ask what post position the horse has drawn. If the answer is "three", the person leading the horse will be handed the number three to either attach to the bridle or to carry by hand to the paddock.

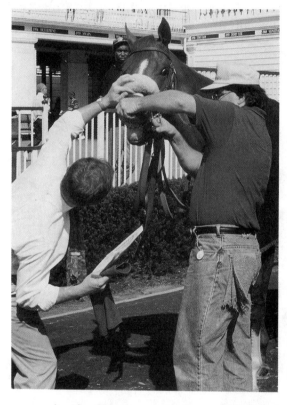

The horse identifier checks the tattoo of all horses entered in the race before they reach the saddling paddock.
Photo by Les Sellnow

As the horse enters the paddock, the second official with which it will have contact is the identifier. This person will have a list of all horses entered in that race. Beside each name will be the number tattooed into the animal's upper lip and its identifying markings.

The individual leading the horse will stop the animal at the identifier who will check the number and compare it with the information on his sheet. From there the horse goes into the saddling paddock. At this point we can lead the youngster around the oval walking ring in front of the saddling stalls or we can lead it directly to a stall to await saddling.

I prefer to place the horse in the stall and let it stand quietly instead of walking around. Horses are creatures of habit. If they get used to standing quietly in a stall, they'll do so. If they are conditioned to being led about, they will get used to that. The only problem with being led about is that the more they are allowed to move about, the more they want to and sometimes you have trouble getting them to stand quietly in the stall for saddling.

Again, I equate it to people. If you are a nervous person and get into a tense situation, one way to calm yourself is to sit quietly and do something that will take your mind from whatever is bothering you. If you walk back and forth in frenzied fashion, you are simply going to make yourself more nervous. It's the same with a horse before a race. If it has been conditioned to stand quietly in its stall with a groom and trainer it trusts, there is a much better chance of it remaining calm than if it is being led around the walking ring where it sees and hears even more strange sights and sounds that stimulate additional anxiety.

Though the young prospect is getting its first look at a crowd of people, it still isn't apt to become too concerned at this point unless it is nervous and skittish by nature. After all, the horse was here once before and then was led back to the barn.

Suddenly, that changes. A strange man comes into the stall carrying a jockey's saddle. This is the jockey's valet, the person charged with the responsibility of helping the trainer place the jockey's personal gear on the horse.

105

Working together, the trainer and the valet saddle the horse.

Once the horse is saddled, the paddock judge comes by to check out the young prospect. He will take note of what type of bit we're using, whether we have blinkers and, if so, what kind, whether the horse is wearing bandages, whether we are using a tongue tie and any other equipment with which this horse has been outfitted.

The next time we run the youngster, the paddock master will compare that list with what the horse is carrying the second time out. Unless we have sought and obtained approval from the starter and the steward to change equipment, the horse should be outfitted exactly the same the second time out as it was in the first race.

A steady pony and a calm soothing pony rider can keep the young racehorse calm and steady on its way to the gate. *Photo by Les Sellnow*

Now, the jockey comes to the saddling stall and the young horse realizes beyond doubt that this is going to be an extra-special day. The youngster still isn't sure what is going on, but the excitement in the air that it first felt when being led into the saddling paddock is increasing.

It's time for the youngster to have something of a security blanket at this point and I like to provide it with a pony horse from our barn. This is an animal that has been used as a steadying influence on the youngster when it first came to the track. I might even go so far as to have the pony rider be the exercise rider that normally rides the youngster in the mornings. This is a case where familiarity of pony horse and rider can have a definite calming influence during a stressful time.

The 12 youngsters are emerging onto the track in front of a grandstand where people are moving about, laughing, talking and the voice of the public address announcer is coming over the loudspeakers listing runners and other information. At a time when the young horse wants to be dancing about in excitement, it is being asked to walk calmly and in a straight line for the post parade.

Finally, the post parade is over and the jockey gallops the horse around the track to get it warmed up. Now, the tension mounts for horse, owner and trainer.

They are approaching the gate.

It's post time.

If the young prospect, for whom we have such high hopes, had the misfortune of drawing the first or second post position in a 12-horse field of babies, it might have a long wait in the gate as the starters struggle to get all of these inexperienced youngsters in line. Some will load easily, others that are becoming stressed by the excitement will balk and may even have to be pushed in.

Finally, they are all in.

The bell rings.

The gates fly open.

The announcer declares, "They're off!"

If you are a normal first-time owner, your heart is in your mouth at this point.

There is nothing more exciting than a horse race, especially if you own one of the runners.

Just that quick, it's over. They've come thundering down the stretch and one of them is carrying your colors.

They sweep under the wire. There are both cheers and moans from the crowd of bettors. Among the owners, one is ecstatic. Maybe it's you. Some are satisfied, some are between satisfied and dissatisfied with what happened and some are just downright angry because their horse lost.

There is only one winner.

That's horse racing.

If your horse is the one that came in first, the trainer will be more than happy to escort you to the winner's circle to pose for a photograph.

As an owner, however, your prime concern should be whether the horse ran well, win or lose, and whether it came out of the race injury-free and with a good attitude.

The aftermath of a race is a time for the trainer and barn crew to keep the youngster under close surveillance. If it finished in the middle of the pack, it may very well be allowed to return immediately to the barn. However, if it won or was second in an exacta race or third in a trifecta where bettors wager on the order of the first and second place or first, second and third, respectively, the youngster will get a new experience. It will go to the detention barn where a urine sample will be taken. Some jurisdictions also may call for blood and/or saliva tests, but all of them test the urine.

Water for the horse to drink and for bathing will be available at the detention barn and its groom and members of the barn crew will be there. Once the horse urinates and a sample has been caught for testing, a barn official will sign a form stating that a urine sample has been obtained and someone from the barn will sign a card verifying that he or she observed the sample being caught and that it was indeed from the horse he or she was handling. The horse is then allowed to return to its stall.

(The urine sample is halved, with one-half being sent to a testing laboratory to learn if any illegal drugs are present. The other half is stored and can be tested at a private laboratory of the trainer's choosing as a double-check in case illegal drugs are reported in the sample tested by the

If the horse finishes "in the money," it is taken to the detention barn where urine, blood or saliva tests are given. *Photo by Les Sellnow*

laboratory chosen by the racing commission.)

Once back at the barn, we might want to bathe this horse again and cool it out even more. Before all that, however, we will want a veterinarian to examine the young prospect endoscopically to learn whether lung or airway damage is evident. This is an extra expense to the owner, but it does a lot to tell the trainer whether the breathing apparatus is functioning normally. With an endoscope, the veterinarian can literally peer into the horse's breathing apparatus to learn whether it bled or whether previously undetected mucous in the lungs clogged the airways.

By "scoping" immediately after the race, I can get a good reading on why the horse performed as it did, good or bad. If I don't "scope", I'm just guessing and I might make a serious mistake in deciding what the next step in training and racing should be.

I like the endoscopic examination to be given as soon as possible after a race. Some detention centers will allow an outside veterinarian to come in and "scope" a horse and others

Immediately after the race, the horse is "scoped" to see if there is any lung or airway damage.
Photo by Les Sellnow

won't. If we are lucky enough to have one of the top horses in a race, we must work within the detention barn's requirements.

Back at the barn, we also want to take a good look at the horse's eyes because if it was running anywhere except in front the entire race, it is going to have been struck in the face by dirt. If we can't clear the dirt and debris from around the eyes with just a saline solution, it's time to have a veterinarian in to examine them.

At the barn we will let the horse relax and totally cool out. If there is grass near the barn, we might let it graze for a time before taking it back to the stall. At the stall, we will allow it to have hay and water and we will "do up" the legs. Once the horse has cooled out, we will rub each leg with alcohol and put light bandages on them. The purpose is to stimulate circulation.

About three hours after the race, the horse is fed its full ration of grain.

The next morning we will examine the young prospect very closely. We'll remove the bandages and take it up to the track for a light training session. We might jog for a mile to let it limber up those sore muscles or we might even gallop.

We'll return to the barn and put the horse up in a two-day poultice. We purchase a commercial poultice that is designed to remove heat and inflammation from the legs. If the horse shows signs of lameness, we'll call in the veterinarian for advice before doing anything.

During the two days the poultice is on, the horse will be hand walked around the shedrow each morning and will spend the rest of the time in the stall.

On the third day, the poultice is washed off and we will take another hard look at the legs.

If the young prospect has come through all of our examinations with flying colors, it is time to make plans for the next steps in the training program.

Chapter Nine

Staying the Course

The race is over and you, as a new owner, are very happy. For sake of discussion, let's say that your two-year-old didn't win, but finished second. You're on a high. Finishing second is mighty good, you reason.

You are elated because you know this horse is going to be a great one and it's just a matter of another race or two before you're standing in the winner's circle. Perhaps someone has even approached you and offered to buy your horse for $75,000, a nifty quick profit on your $40,000 purchase. Of course, you will turn down that offer because you've already gotten a financial return on your investment through a share of the purse.

Instead, you're riding so high that you decide the thing to do is to buy more horses.

After all, you reason, it's easy. You went to the sale and, with the help of the evaluation crew, picked a young prospect that proved to be everything you expected and even more.

So, you are ready to take a bigger plunge into the Thoroughbred business. You have just experienced a wonderful emotional high and you want more.

It's time to buy, you tell the trainer.

Wrong.

You shouldn't buy more horses right now.

Now is not the time to invest additional money. Now is

the time to stick with the original game plan and budget, both of which were established prior to last September's sale. If you buy more horses, your expenses will increase and then you're over budget and you've only been in the business a matter of months.

There are several reasons for being cautious at this point. First of all, one good race doesn't make, or break, a horse's career. Remember, this was the youngster's first race. It might also be the best race it will ever run. We hope not, but it could be. It's happened to many horses. They're never again as good as they were that first time out of the gate.

Instead of making a greater financial commitment, now is the time to sit back and study the young prospect. It's more important to assess how the horse came out of the race than to revel in how well it did when running. Here's where you must lean on the trainer's expertise and be guided by what he or she observes and interprets.

To learn how the young prospect fares in the days immediately following that first race, we are going to observe it closely.

Remember the four traits? Mental toughness, ability, soundness and a good immune system?

The trait we'll concentrate on right after a race is mental toughness. Obviously, we'll check the horse very carefully for soundness, but our chief concern is this: how did the race affect it mentally?

Frequently, the soundness and mental traits overlap. Every young horse is going to be a little stiff and sore after racing. I compare them to young human athletes. High school and college basketball or football players are going to have stiff muscles after a strenuous game, but often there's a difference in how they react. Some will moan and groan about how terrible they feel and how much pain they're in while others will walk right through the discomfort without giving it a second thought.

It's the same with horses. Some of them have a high pain and discomfort threshold and others have a threshold that's very low. Two horses might have the same degree of stiffness, but one will gimp along while the other will ignore the discomfort and move out freely as though nothing's wrong.

It's adjustment time again.

We've been adjusting to the young horse's needs all along. Now, in the wake of its first race, we must adjust even more. But first, we must know what those needs are.

The horse with the low pain threshold, for example, shouldn't be exercised with the same vigor right after a race as the horse that pays no attention to a little soreness and stiff muscles. The horse with the low pain threshold might need to be just walked around the shedrow for a few days after the poultices come off while the other can be ridden to the track and jogged or even galloped.

This doesn't mean that the horse with the low pain threshold is going to be a poor racehorse. It might be a very good one if the trainer is capable of adjusting to its needs for additional rest and a bit of coddling.

Again, just like with people, some horses are fast healers and others aren't. One person might suffer a broken leg and it will knit in no time. Another person will suffer the same fracture, but spend many more months before the bone heals and becomes strong again.

Know your horse and adjust.

While tolerance of pain is not the most telling factor, it's been my experience, generally speaking, that good horses have a mind that overrides pain. Your lesser horses will have a mind that pain overrides.

But that, again, is not an absolute.

The way in which our young prospect finished the race may have a lot to do with its mental recovery. Was it leading

115

right down to the last sixteenth of a mile, only to be out of energy and have the rest of the field sweep past? Or was it laying about sixth in the pack of 12 and then closed with a rush that carried it past all but the winning horse?

Hopefully, your young $40,000 prospect was in the latter category - a horse that was still gaining ground when it went beneath the wire. Running first and then having the field sweep past with clods of dirt hitting it in the face might prove to be a devastating experience for a young horse that was still giving its all at that point, but whose energy tank had run dry.

To evaluate your young prospect and its mental condition, let's return to the morning after the race. As I've said, I like to take a horse to the track and at least jog it on the day after a race. I don't want it lying around the stall, getting stiff and sore. Exercise is the best antidote for stiffness. I don't want to stress the horse, just walk and jog it to get the circulation going.

How the horse reacts on that first trip to the track the morning after a race is going to be telling. You want to see a colt or filly that's ready and eager to go to the track. And when it gets there, you hope it will jog along nice and relaxed, taking everything in, but not getting excited as it casually limbers up its stiff muscles but demonstrates no signs of unsoundness.

If this is what happens with your young prospect, it's cause for rejoicing because we now have our four necessary traits all functioning in a positive way. The horse has come through the race without mental or emotional trauma; it has remained sound; its immune system continues to function as it should, and the youngster demonstrated ability during the race itself.

Ah, we tell ourselves, we just might have a racehorse here.

All the necessary traits are in order and the way the

youngster came flying down the lane at the end of the race brings to mind that wonderful five-letter word.

Class.

Only racing competition can tell us if our prospect has class. It's too early to make the declaration after only one outing, but the indicators from that race are all positive at this point.

If, on the other hand, the young prospect gets agitated when we go to the track on the morning after the race and comes back to the barn nervous and sweaty, we know that the race produced mental stress. Three traits might be functioning as we desire, but one of them - mental toughness - is now a question mark.

We must be thinking about training adjustments. It would be foolhardy to train this nervous young prospect exactly as we will the horse that went to the track calm and confident the day after the race.

If the nervous horse left all of the food placed in its tub the evening of race day and has sore ankles or a strained stifle to boot the next morning, our problems mount and the need for proper adjustment to the training regimen gains added importance.

(Food consumption is a significant identifier of post-race stress. It's not unusual for a young horse to fail to clean up a complete ration after a race, but if most of the food is uneaten, it is usually because the horse is suffering from stress).

Remember, what we have seen in the two above comparisons still has not told us that one of these prospects will be a great horse and the other won't. Only additional training and racing will reveal that. For the moment, however, we know that one prospect is right where we want it and the other isn't.

The trainer must regulate the training regimens in the upcoming days and weeks to fit each of these horse's needs.

Adjust.

Adjust.

Adjust.

It is impossible to over-emphasize the necessity of a trainer adjusting to an individual horse's needs.

Now that we have assessed how the young prospect reacted the first day back in training following a race, it's time to re-evaluate how the horse finished.

If it was on the lead and then got "buried" at the end and finished back in the pack and on the day following the race, demonstrated all the classic signs of stress and nervousness, we might be looking at a questionable prospect.

If, however, the horse that led and then came up short at the end, showed no sign of stress or unsoundness the next day, and was eager to get back to the track, we might be looking at a talented youngster that just wasn't quite fit enough. Nothing to worry about here. This two-year-old is going to do nothing but get better. Forget where it finished. It really doesn't matter at this point.

Of course, from my point of view, the best scenario of all is for the youngster to have been gaining ground at the wire and to show no ill effects the next day. That tells me this horse withstood the dirt hitting it in the face in the early stages of the race and that it probably had to work its way between horses to get running room.

That takes mental toughness.

There's no simple mathematical formula for evaluating these young horses after one race. The evaluation involves close observation and study. The trainer must be able to "read" what that horse is feeling and react accordingly.

Let's go back to the youngster that closed strongly in that first race and came through it unscathed mentally or physically. It's time to look into its future.

How much time elapses between its first race and the

second will be dependent on how the horse trains and what races are available. Time is not of the essence at this point. It's as Jack Van Berg says, "Time is only relevant if you're in jail."

After the young prospect is ready, and again there is no magic formula to determine when it will be ready, we will give it a light half mile work. This might be a week after the race or it might be 10 days or more. A light half mile work would be going the half mile in about 50 seconds or better on a fast track. The trainer will have to feel when the horse is ready for this work and, again, that will vary widely.

If the youngster is ready and eager to run during the half-mile work and is still showing a willing eagerness down the home stretch, we might want to be thinking about a second race in about ten days to two weeks.

Much of the decision making concerning when you run a young horse again will be determined by what your plans are, especially if it's a top prospect. You might be running it back in a couple weeks or you might not enter it again for a month. It all depends on the master plan.

You, as the owner, might want to experience, as soon as possible, that high of again watching your horse fly down the lane, gaining ground with every stride. That may not be the best thing for the youngster. The good trainer will instead be looking four to six months into the future and be planning just how to reach that point with a sound and successful horse. Maybe the youngster shows the kind of potential that makes us think Breeders' Cup that fall. If that's the case, we have to plan carefully to get it into the right races along the way preparatory to meeting that goal.

A two-year-old normally will not race more than seven times and a great many will get only two to six starts, if they start at all.

As a trainer, once you know you have a good horse,

don't destroy it by entering every race that comes along. Pick your spots and develop the horse slowly and carefully. Always give it a chance to exhibit its class in races where it's fit, fresh and eager.

Don't be in a hurry.

We also must give consideration to the company in which the horse competed that first time out when doing our evaluation. In Unbridled's first two-year-old race, he was six or seven lengths out of it at the half mile pole. He then circled the field on the turn and won by 10 lengths. That was a good win, but what made it even more significant was the strength of the field.

The horse that finished second went on to be a stakes contender that earned a half million dollars and the horse that finished third, Home At Last, which I trained, earned a million dollars.

Home At Last had been running ahead of Unbridled early in the race, but wound up third. Here was a case where being passed and finishing third had no harmful effects. Home At Last came out of that race in great shape, mentally and physically and went on to be very successful. In fact, he beat Unbridled in the Super Derby when they both were three.

What I'm saying here is that you don't evaluate your horse only by how well it did in good company as opposed to weaker, but it can be a strong indicator. A horse that is lacking in class might be a barn burner against weaker opposition, but may run very poorly when matched against a class field.

Now, we have reached the point with our positive young prospect where we know what our goals are. We evaluated the horse, observed it, tested it and everything has remained positive. Let's say that we think it's a good enough prospect that we should be aiming for Breeders' Cup in the fall. From now on the horse's entire training regimen and the races scheduled for it will be conducted with that goal in mind.

As we go along, we will adjust, adjust, adjust, as we get to know the horse better and better. And every time we make an adjustment, we'll step back to evaluate how the horse accepts the adjustment.

By the time the youngster has been in five races, we're going to have a pretty good handle on everything about this horse. About all that we won't know is just how well it will do against a full field of class competitors.

Where will we find that out for sure?

Will it be in the two-year-old classic at Breeders' Cup?

Or will it be at Churchill Downs on the first Saturday in May of the horse's three-year-old-year?

Do we truly have a Derby horse here?

How far will this young prospect take us?

The excitement that builds as a good young horse develops, brings the best of highs. As an owner-trainer team, we know we've brought this horse along with a training program that has yielded steady, positive development.

This is pure horse racing excitement.

But what about the young prospect that succumbed to stress in the wake of the first race? When do we run it back?

The answer is as simple as it's complicated. As soon as the horse settles down and is ready. Which, of course, begs the question: when is it ready?

We already know that we are going to have to go slowly with this horse. It may need several days in the shedrow just to settle down and relax. From there we'll ease the horse back into the training track mainstream with a lot of jogging and, later, galloping.

As we sense that the horse is relaxing both in the stall and on the track, it's time to take it back to the starting gate. We won't pressure the horse; just move it into the gate and let stand quietly and relax. When the horse has passed this

121

hurdle and is not showing signs of nervousness or stress, it is time to give it a half mile work.

I'll tell the exercise rider to just sit quietly on the horse and apply no pressure. If it takes 52 or 53 seconds to cover the half mile, that's fine, as long as the horse remains relaxed.

Once the horse is cleaning up a full ration of food, is getting its bloom back, going to the track and through the starting gate with confidence, it's time for its second race. This may have taken a couple weeks and it may have taken a couple months.

Remember, at this point, time is irrelevant. What matters is having the horse in a healthy frame of mind. With this horse you can't plan two, three, four or six months in advance as you can with the confident prospect. Your planning can only involve getting it mentally and physically ready for a second race.

All the while we are getting ready for the second race, we will continue looking for clues from the first race that will help us adjust. Maybe, for example, the jockey hustled the horse out of the gate quickly in that first race and took the horse immediately to the front. It may have gotten frustrated when the other runners came up on it and that brought on the stress that we've been trying to overcome.

This time, we might tell the jockey to let the youngster break sharply out of the gate, but not to be in a hurry from that point on. Just let it run easy in whatever position seems comfortable, we'll tell him or her. Then, when the jockey feels the youngster get stronger on the bit, it will be time to let it make a move on the leaders.

This is where good communication between a trainer and jockey is important. As the trainer, you will tell the jockey to "just sit on him." This means that once out of the gate and running, the jockey won't ask anything of the horse. He'll just sit there and wait for its confidence to build. When that happens, we will have told the jockey, "Just ride your race and make your move when you're ready."

We will also have told the jockey to be ready for the reverse. If the youngster comes out of the gate and loses it and

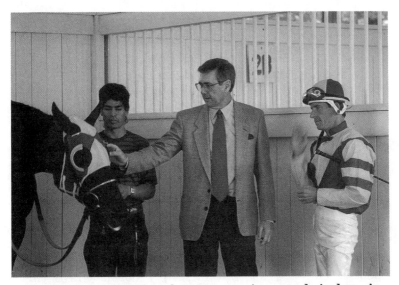

Good communication between trainer and jockey is important. Here Carl and Craig Perret confer before a race at Saratoga. *Photo by Les Sellnow*

is looking for a way out, the jockey has to take a different tactic. If that happens, we'll have told the jockey, "send him."

To me a horse is losing it and looking for a way out when it starts trying to get out of the pack in whatever way it can, except by running straight forward with speed. When that happens, it is time for the jockey to perhaps use his whip to get this youngster focused on what we are asking it to do.

If scenario one happens in the second race - the youngster relaxes and makes a run for the lead down the home stretch - we know we have overcome some problems and once again are working with a good prospect. Our spirits are up.

If, however, the horse shows no desire to run and seeks

only to escape, it's another, not so pleasant, matter. The horse has flat told us it doesn't want to run.

Time for another adjustment.

This time the adjustment might be major. If we decide the horse has talent, but just lacks mental maturity, it might be time to send it back to the farm and turn it out for several months, bringing it back into training for a three-year-old campaign.

We still may have the makings for a successful racehorse, but we know that success won't come as a two-year-old. The good news is that the horse has gone through training and is still sound. It just isn't mentally strong, at least at this stage of its development.

Maybe as a three-year-old, it will do better going long or maybe we will give it a try on the turf. If the horse is bred well and the owners are committed to giving the horse another chance, our decision is easy. Just give the horse some time off and bring it back as a three-year-old.

If, however, after two or three times out, the young prospect is showing us that it simply doesn't have the four necessary traits to be a successful racehorse, we have to start thinking about other alternatives. If it is getting even more temperamental, showing more signs of unsoundness, less ability than we might have thought and perhaps even a breakdown of the immune system, it's time to consider selling the horse or perhaps entering it in claiming races where the competition is not as tough.

By now it's September which is a time when people often are buying horses. As an owner, you might have to take a loss, or you might not, depending on what someone else sees or wants from your prospect. Let us assume you have been looking for a horse that can compete in first-class allowance races. Your prospect may not be able to do that, but someone else may be looking for a horse that will be competitive in lesser competition. So, sale by private treaty is a possibility.

If there are no prospects for private purchase, you might want to simply enter the horse in a claiming race. When you do this, magic can happen. A horse that couldn't handle a higher level of competition will often bloom when run against horses with less talent.

Let's use our boxers for another analogy. Remember the amateur that we sent against Mohammed Ali? After a couple beatings, we couldn't even get him back into the ring. Now, if we let him return to the amateur level, he might become a tiger in the ring again. These guys are easy compared to Muhammad Ali.

That's the way it is with horses. The horse that couldn't compete against class runners might just tear up the field in a claiming race. If that happens, someone else is bound to claim it, thinking that this horse can move right back up to allowance competition.

Sometimes it can, but more often than not it cannot. Those traits, or lack of them, that held it back in the first place are still there and likely will rise to the surface again when the horse is put against stronger competition. Oh, the horse might turn in one good race in the faster company, but then what I call cellular memory kicks in. The horse remembers what happened when it had to face this kind of company in the past and it reverts back to a stress-filled competitor that ultimately is finishing in the back of the pack. It may never achieve success beyond the claiming level.

I believe that every great human athlete competes at a level that transcends his or her ability. They rise above themselves in the heat of intense competition and give 110 percent.

So do horses.

The horse that we dropped to the claiming level where it's successful and then is brought back to allowance races, may give you that 110 percent one time out and finish third. Then, when the cellular memory kicks in and the horse realizes it gave all it had and more and still couldn't pass the leaders, it normally stops giving 110 percent.

If that horse remains at the allowance level of competition, it will give less and less each time out and finish further and further in the rear of the also-rans.

But, enough of that, back to the youngster that is on the other end of the scale. It has taken us to great heights of excitement, but we may learn there is much more to come.

Chapter 10

The Making of a Winner

To this point, we have been discussing fictional prospects, what might happen with them and the ways in which we try to adjust in their training regimens. It's time to get more specific as to how this approach works in a real life situation. There is only one way for me to do that - discuss a horse with which I was involved from beginning to end in his racing career.

Unbridled.

For me, the Unbridled story begins in 1987 when Tartan Farms and John Nerud dispersed their Thoroughbreds. In a way, I suppose, it actually began much earlier because I had been involved for some time as a trainer for Tartan Farms and through them, Genter Stables. As a result, I knew the breeding program and what to expect from it.

However, the man responsible for breeding Unbridled was John A. Nerud, a man for whom I have the greatest respect and from whom I've learned much.

Earlier we discussed pedigree and the role it plays in the evaluation process when we're selecting yearlings with racing potential. I think John Nerud's description of the matings leading to Unbridled is a classic example of how thoughtful breeding decisions can result in something more than a good pedigree - a winning racehorse.

Unbridled is by Fappiano and out of the Le Fabuleux daughter, Gana Facil, a mare, who though not black type, was an allowance winner of about $100,000.

Here's is Mr. Nerud's explanation of the breeding program that produced Unbridled, as told to David Heckerman of The Blood-Horse:

"We bred Aspidistra to Buckpasser the first year that he retired to stud (1968) and we got Magic, who never raced but had some bottom in her for sure, because she was by Buckpasser. She was a big mare and I bred her to In Reality, and I got a medium-sized mare in Charedi, who could run seven-eighths of a mile and was close to stakes quality, though she never actually won a stakes.

"I thought at that point that the family needed some more bottom so I bred Charedi to Le Fabuleux, a Wild Risk horse who was another stamina influence and a good sire of broodmares. We came up with Gana Facil, who was a good allowance winner--again close to a stakes mare, but not quite. So I said now we have bred bottom back into the line, so I'll go to speed in Fappiano, and that's how we got Unbridled."

A classic master of the art of breeding at work, producing a beautiful combination of stamina and speed.

Unbridled.

When I first saw the colt he didn't look like all that much. He was a long-legged, gangly weanling at the Tartan dispersal sale. Likely, if he'd been in a commercial stable he wouldn't have gone to the auction until he was a yearling, but this was a dispersal, so everything sold. The Genter stable had decided to purchase Gana Facil and thought it a good idea to buy her colt as well so they could get an early look at the type of runners she was producing.

Unbridled sold for $70,000.

He was sent to Mike O'Farrell's Ocala Stud in Florida and in September of his yearling year, he began the breaking schedule we've already described. Right from the start he showed potential, with a couple of the necessary traits surfacing. He was a sound colt, had an excellent mind, stayed healthy and all the way along, provided hints that he had ability.

In April, the Genter stable yearlings were split among the three trainers with whom they were affiliated at the time. I was one of the three and Unbridled came to us in April of 1989 while we were at Keeneland.

He was still gangly as a two-year-old. One of the things that impressed me about this colt from the very beginning was

"One of the things that impressed me about this colt (Unbridled) from the very beginning was that he liked people." C. Nafzger

Photo by Robin Ann Berry

that he liked people. He would do whatever you asked of him and seemed to enjoy it. He would go up to the track, gallop and come back a happy horse.

When we started his gate work, the same was true. He didn't get excited or rattled in the gate. He would do whatever we wanted - stand there quietly, walk through or gallop out.

129

Nothing bothered him.

As he became more fit, the ability trait began to surface even more. He could run with the other horses in his age group.

Now we had all four traits in place - a good mind, soundness, an excellent immune system and ability. We would find out if class would surface when we started him the first time.

As his training progressed, we noticed another peculiarity. When he was breezing with another horse, it was almost as if he were taking care of it. He would run alongside the other horse, twitching his ears and watching it. He would never grab the bit and try to run off; he never got rank and tried to throw in a surge of speed and beat the other horse. It didn't matter what the pace was, he'd just stay even, watching that horse and twitching his ears. He loved what he was doing, but he was very kind to the other horse while he was doing it.

As his training progressed, he began to bloom. He muscled up and became more coordinated. And it didn't matter who we breezed him with; he was always the dominant colt. That doesn't mean he was faster than the others because we never let them breeze to see which one could get the lead. But, every time we breezed, Unbridled was always playing with the colt beside him in kindly fashion. It didn't matter whether we had him on the rail or on the outside, he'd just be running along, tracking that other colt with his ears twitching. Having fun.

After we received his gate approval, it was time to get him to a race. In his last work before that inaugural race, I had jockey Mike Smith up on Unbridled and we breezed him with another good colt. It wasn't really fast, five-eighths in about 1:01 and 3, not a black letter work, but just a good sharp breeze and they galloped out strong in about 1:15 for six furlongs.

I remember that morning well because it's where I first publicly expressed the belief that this horse was going to be extra special.

"What do you think of him, Mike?" I asked.

"He's nice," Mike said.

"If this horse can run like I think he can," I said, "with his attitude, if he can get around two turns, he could be my Derby horse."

We were at Arlington Park now and four days later Unbridled had his first start in a six-furlong maiden race. My instructions to Mike that day were about the same as they are to every jockey who rides a two-year-old in its first race: "Get him out of the gate, get him focused, let him settle, don't rush him, just let him stride and see where he is." Unknown to me at the time was the fact that this approach was to become this colt's trademark.

Unbridled broke well and Mike just let him settle into his stride. By the time he reached the half-mile pole, he was about six lengths from the lead, but now he was really collected. Around the turn they were two wide. Mike just sort of tightened on him and from the three-eighths pole to the quarter pole, he circled the field and at the quarter pole he took the lead. Mike just hand rode him and finished 10 lengths in front. As I mentioned earlier, the second and third place horses were both class runners who went on to become stakes winners. By whatever barometer we chose to use, Unbridled's class had surfaced.

I thought, well, for sure we have a sprinter, but can he go around two turns?

We next entered him in a stakes race that we thought he'd win. He didn't. It was six furlongs and on a fast track. He finished third, seven lengths behind the winner.

I didn't catch on to the fact right away that this horse

didn't like being rushed. We ran him back in the Arch Ward stakes at Arlington. It was a slick, muddy track. He ran third again, beaten by 18 or 20 lengths.

Two thoughts went through my mind immediately after that race. First, the colt didn't like the mud. That was now indisputable. Second, we were using the wrong approach in our race strategy. We were hustling him out of the gate so he would be close to the front-runners. I was still convinced he had ability because he finished third in both races and was only galloping.

Time to adjust.

We looked around for a race that would be right for him and where we could employ the new strategy of letting him come from off the pace. There was a nice race at Canterbury Downs in Minnesota that seemed to fit the bill perfectly so we entered him there. It was a one-mile $100,000 stakes race for two-year-olds and it would be around two turns.

This time, I told Mike to just sit on him and see if he would close. As the race unfolded, the colt dropped back seven, eight lengths, but when Mike asked him, he came running and finished second by half a length. He came out of that race in fine fashion. He was relaxed and cleaned up his food that night.

In fact, the only time he ever came out of races a bit nervous were those first two on the mud.

Up to this point, we didn't have to worry about a specific schedule as there were plenty of races either in Chicago or nearby, such as the one at Canterbury. Now, that was beginning to change. We had to look further ahead.

Unbridled was nominated for Breeders' Cup, so we decided that he should go to Florida, run in the Stallion Stakes in October and, two weeks later, the Breeders' Cup.

We were having trouble getting air transportation, so decided to make the trip by van in easy stages. We shipped from Minnesota back to Chicago, freshened him by just backing off on the training pressure for a few days, then galloped, put in a light breeze, then vanned him to Keeneland where we did about the same thing.

From there we shipped to Calder, gave him a week to adjust, worked him once over the track and then ran him at a mile and a sixteenth. He ran well, finishing second and was closing, just flying, at the end.

At that time, Calder had the old track with the artificial Tartan beneath the surface and a horse really needed a race to get the feel of it. He hadn't had the requisite race, but had run well. I was satisfied.

Unfortunately, when we 'scoped' Unbridled after that race, we discovered that he'd bled. It was decision time again. Should we take a chance and run him in the Breeders' Cup or should we put him on the bleeders' list? There were 12 days between the Stallion Stakes and Breeders' Cup. When you put a horse on the bleeders' list, he can't run for 14 days. So, if we were to run in the Breeders' Cup, it would be without medication.

We put him on the Bleeders' List. I felt it was the only sound decision. Because he had bled, I knew we'd have to back off on his training or the stress of continued work could cause the problem to recur and, perhaps, worsen. And, if we backed off on his training, he wouldn't be ready for Breeders' Cup anyway.

Adjustment.

I was now convinced. Unbridled could win the Kentucky Derby. We sat down and mapped out a plan, complete with some options in case of problems along the way, that would put us in the gate at Churchill Downs the first Saturday in May.

Unbridled had all the traits going for him - mental, soundness, ability and a good immune system. And there was something else. This horse just simply didn't make mistakes. All of us around him did, but he didn't. And he just kept getting better each time out. He was growing in confidence. Every time he went back to the race track he was more sure of himself. He built on every race he ran. Something else had surfaced early on and was unmistakable.

Class.

Under our plan, his next race, the last as a two-year-old,

People began noticing Unbridled after his five-length victory in the What A Pleasure stakes.

Photo by Jean Raftery

would be in December. It was the What A Pleasure stakes. If he did well there, we'd go to the Tropical Park Derby. The Tropical Park Derby would propel him into the Fountain Of Youth. From the Fountain Of Youth, we'd go to the Florida Derby. If all was still going well at that point, we would have

134

three alternatives - the Jim Beam, which is four weeks prior to the Kentucky Derby; the Bluegrass Stakes, which is three weeks before the Derby or the Arkansas Derby two weeks before the Kentucky Derby.

We also had alternate plans all along the way so that if something went wrong, we could use a race here or there as substitutes, but still with the Kentucky Derby as the goal.

The $50,000 What A Pleasure stakes, run at a mile and a sixteenth, was our springboard for the campaign ahead. It proved to be a good one. There was a quality field and Unbridled dominated them, finishing five lengths in front. It was here, for the first time, that the racing public really began taking notice of this colt.

His next race would be the Tropical Park Derby on January 14, 1990. His training schedule at this point in his career involved a lot of galloping and light works at both a half-mile and five-eighths. He loved to work five-eighths, picking up the pace as he went, finishing the last quarter in 24.1 or 23.4.

How often did we breeze him? There was no set pattern. We breezed him when he asked for it. Here again, we're back to getting inside a horse's mind. This was not a colt for which one established a set routine and didn't vary it. You could just feel when he was bursting with energy and wanted to run. He'd get cockier and cockier. You could also tell by the way he was galloping. Unbridled would gallop the mile anywhere from 2:03 or 2:04 to 2:15. As he got sharper and sharper, the times would drop and he would be hitting that mile in 2:03. He would come off the track just bouncing.

At that point, we would give him the five-eighths work that he really loved. On the other hand, if he happened to be a bit sluggish and losing his bounce, we would change the tempo and work him a light half, just to wake him up.

He would train as hard as you asked, but he was at his

best when he trained light. Unbridled would flat tell you what he wanted. His ears would just be twitching when he was fit and feeling full of run. All I, as the trainer, had to do was watch, listen and adjust accordingly.

There's an old expression I like to use in describing Unbridled when he was getting fit and ready. He'd hit the ground and go up into the air and the ground would run under him. It wasn't as though he were pulling himself over the ground, it was more as though the ground were coming to him.

He had another trait that his sire also possessed. He 'clocked' his riders during works. He never just took the bit and ran. Not ever. He always waited for the rider to tell him when to move and then he'd explode. And he knew when that should be. You could see him twitching his ears, tensing those muscles in anticipation of a signal that he not only knew would come, but at what point in the work it would be given.

I remember watching Fappiano one morning shortly after I had gone to work for Mr. Nerud and Tartan Farm.

Mr. Nerud said, "Watch this colt work. He can run."

Fappiano was clocking his rider, who was sitting quietly on him. The horse was waiting for that rider to cluck or move his hands, and you knew that at that moment he would explode with a burst of speed. Some years later, I would see the exact same trait in his son, Unbridled. A good horse will wait on the rider. He will be going fast, but he will wait for the signal before he gives that extra surge.

Watching a good rider work Unbridled was like poetry in motion. They would be so in synch. The rider just sitting there. Unbridled running with pure grace and rhythm. Ears twitching. Waiting. Waiting. Waiting. The signal, ever so subtle, and a sudden explosion of speed and raw power.

The jockeys that breezed him prior to his races - Mike Smith, Craig Perret, Jose Velez - would come off the track after a work like that, just grinning.

136

I've mentioned frequently that those of us who comprised Unbridled's human team made mistakes. A major mistake was made in the Tropical Derby, Unbridled's first race as a three-year-old. Things got off to a bad start because Jose Velez, the jockey who was supposed to be up on Unbridled, had a bad spill the day before and was in the hospital. I called Craig Perret and he came in to ride the colt.

It was a race we all - owners, trainer, jockey, barn crew - thought Unbridled could win. The big fear was that some speed horse would jump out in front and steal it. The decision was to keep Unbridled up with the leaders right out of the gate. That's just what Craig did. Kept him laying about number two. As they turned to head for home, we all were waiting for Unbridled to make his move. It never came. He finished fifth, beaten by almost six lengths.

What we had done was impose our will on this horse to run the kind of race he had already told us he didn't want to run. We took away his rhythm and imposed ours on him.

It didn't work.

After the race was over, there was a meeting between trainer and owners. The confidence of the owners and some of his backers was shaken. They wondered if he truly was Derby material. I told them there was nothing wrong with the horse. He was still just as good as we'd thought. We were the ones who had made the mistake because we took away what he wanted to do and tried to make him bend to our will.

It was at this meeting that the pattern was set for the rest of Unbridled's racing career. I said that, as trainer, it was my decision that this horse would never again be hustled out of the gate to run with the leaders. He would come from off the pace. If a speed horse got up front and speed held, so be it. Then he would get beat. But he would get beat running his race.

Craig came to the barn the next morning. He had been

137

thinking the same thing.

He said, simply: "We did it wrong."

My next goal for Unbridled was the Fountain Of Youth on March 3, a prep race for the Florida Derby. I figured that if he didn't do well in the Fountain Of Youth and the Florida Derby, I would be forced to admit he wasn't the "big" horse and we would have to go hunting some lesser races. But, in the meantime I was going to remain convinced that this was a colt that could win the Run for the Roses.

As we prepared for the Fountain Of Youth, Craig Perret made the decision to ride Rhythm in the race. I called Pat Day and he agreed to ride Unbridled.

It was a race that Unbridled very definitely was capable of winning, but that's horse racing. He got into some unavoidable traffic problems and there was nothing Pat could do about it. When it was time to make his move, there were three horses in front of him and one, that was tiring, was outside of him. Pat was trying to get out, but the jockey on the tiring outside horse was holding his position and Pat and Unbridled couldn't make the move.

About 50 yards from the wire, Pat found a tiny crack of daylight and Unbridled exploded through it. He did everything but physically push that tiring horse out of the way. He shot through the tiny crack of daylight without hitting the other horse and unleashed an awesome closing kick. It was a fantastic surge of speed and power, but it came too late. Shot Gun Scott won it, Smelly was second and Unbridled, third, beaten by only half a length.

In the Fountain Of Youth, Unbridled went off at long odds. But that dramatic burst of speed when he saw daylight caused a whole lot of folks to sit up and take notice. By the time we got to the Florida Derby on March 17, he went off at very close odds, even though the field included a bunch of class horses.

138

The track was dead the day of the mile and one-eighth Florida Derby and there wasn't much speed in the field. Unbridled laid off the pace and closed with a rush to win it by four lengths. However, it was one of the slowest Florida Derbies ever run and, again, a lot of people wrote him off as a Kentucky Derby contender, thinking he was too slow.

That didn't bother me. I knew this colt was going to be a good Derby horse. Once again there was a jockey switch. Pat was committed to riding Summer Squall, a horse with great tactical speed, but Rhythm was out for throat surgery so Craig Perret again was available. (By tactical speed, I mean that Summer Squall could lay right up there near the leaders, just off the pace, and whenever the time was right could explode with an extra burst.)

Once again it was decision time as we looked ahead to the forthcoming three prep races available - the Jim Beam, the Bluegrass and the Arkansas Derby. The Florida Derby was March 17. The Bluegrass Stakes was April 14. Unbridled had been used pretty hard thus far in the campaign, so I figured having about a month before the next race would be just right. We could freshen him a bit, run him in the Bluegrass and then have three weeks to get ready for the Derby.

We shipped him to Keeneland, backed off on his training schedule and after he let us know he was ready for some harder work, got him ready for the Bluegrass. An old problem reared its head.

It rained.

Decision time again.

The Jim Beam, a week earlier, was history. If we didn't run in the Bluegrass, we'd have to ship to Oak Lawn Park and run in the Arkansas Derby which was only two weeks before the Derby. I didn't want to do that, but I also didn't want to run him in the mud. I remembered well that he didn't like a slippery track.

All that being considered, I opted for the Bluegrass and its muddy track.

I told Craig to just let Unbridled run his kind of race and not worry about pressuring him for more than he was willing to give on a muddy track. I said: "When you hit the head of the lane, ask this colt to run and let's see if he can close on Summer Squall. Because, if he can close on Summer Squall on this track, he'll beat him in the Derby. If he can't handle the track, don't worry about it. Let's not get him hurt."

In that race, Unbridled was again off the pace, but not far behind Summer Squall. When Pat asked Summer Squall for run, Craig did the same. Unbridled was closing on Summer Squall when he switched leads in the stretch. I saw Unbridled's head come up when he switched leads and I knew he was not liking that slippery track.

Summer Squall sailed right down the lane and won it. Unbridled ran third.

Wisely, Craig didn't abuse Unbridled for not extending himself in the mud. He rode hard, but he didn't go to the whip. That's the sign of a good jockey. When they feel a horse isn't handling a track, they will never get after them.

Horatio Luro always used to say: "Never squeeze the lemon dry."

Well, we were not going to squeeze the lemon dry in a race over a track that definitely was not to the colt's liking.

The next question was this: how would he come out of a race in the mud? Would he be nervous and edgy like he was after running in the mud as a two-year-old?

He cleaned up all of his food that night. That was a good sign. This colt was going to be ready for the race of his life come the first weekend in May.

Chapter 11

On the Derby Trail

With the Bluegrass behind us, we focused on our goal. The Kentucky Derby. We were able to do so without much pressure from the racing press. They had all fastened on Summer Squall and Mister Frisky as the horses to beat.

It isn't that you don't want to be the favorite because sometimes that means you have the best horse. But, when you are coming into a major race like the Kentucky Derby and you're the favorite, you have everybody in the world wanting to help you. If you aren't the favorite, you have a better chance to do what you want without being pressured.

As a trainer, you soon learn that if you have a good horse, everybody wants to help you train it. If you have a bad one, they let you do it by yourself.

At one point with Unbridled after he won the Derby, one of his connections called to pass on advice from a supposed expert; advice that would help him run even better.

I replied, "I think I'm doing a pretty good job with Unbridled and can get by without any help. But, I've got a horse in the barn named Yellow Medicine that I've done everything I know how to do, and he still can't win a race. I'd like for you to go back and tell that fellow that I'd sure appreciate it if he could help me with Yellow Medicine instead."

Three weeks.

That's what remained between the Bluegrass and the Derby. Just the right amount of time to give you one last chance to correct all the mistakes you have made. What you don't want to learn at this point is that you have overtrained. That puts you in a horrible predicament.

What you are hoping is that you have a horse that just needs to be freshened in the early going of the three weeks and then sharpened shortly before the race itself. During the freshening period, you will keep him on full feed, but will cut back on the pressure of the training sessions. You will want to keep close tabs on his weight. If you can keep him eating good while staying relaxed, he should put on weight. When you take him to the track during a freshening period, you'll do a lot of easy galloping. Let him set his own pace.

Unbridled, as I've mentioned, would gallop anywhere from 2:03 to 2:15 for a mile. The more fit he got, the faster he went. He seemed most comfortable galloping a 2:04 mile. With his stride, he could do it with ease and when he wanted to go at that speed, we let him because if you pulled him, up he would lose his rhythm and travel rough and unevenly.

Rhythm is something a trainer must pay attention to when galloping horses. It doesn't matter at what speed you gallop them, particularly; what matters is that the horse is in rhythm when he gallops. Unbridled seemed to achieve perfect rhythm at 2:04. For another horse it might be 2:10 or even 2:20. The horse will tell you where that rhythm is if you are observant. It's at a point where he's traveling along, looking relaxed, yet with ears pricked forward, enjoying himself. Find where the horse is using himself, but is happy doing it and you will have found his rhythm.

When we breeze a horse during the freshening period, it will likely be a half mile in 52 or 51 seconds. If he's a real fast colt, we might go 49.4 or 50 flat, but we don't demand speed.

If you go five-eighths, which was Unbridled's favorite distance, you'd do it in about 1:03 or a little slower instead of 1:01. He'll be getting his exercise, but he won't be pressured.

You don't reach down and ask him to give you that extra extension, that extra effort. If he's a good colt, he'll come off the track just bouncing after a work like that and, as race day approaches, you can look toward faster works that will sharpen him.

A horse's perfect rhythm is at a point where he is traveling along, looking relaxed yet with ears pricked forward, enjoying himself. Unbridled during a workout prior to the Breeders' Cup *Photo by Dan Johnson*

I repeat Horatio Luro's advice: "Never squeeze a lemon dry."

We hadn't squeezed Unbridled dry to this point. Just the opposite. He was approaching a peak, but hadn't reached it.

All the traits were in order.

He was sound. He came out of one race after another with no physical problems.

He had a good mental attitude. He got more confident with each outing.

He had ability. He had proven that by beating some of the best young horses in the county and running competitively when he didn't win.

His immune system was functioning perfectly. We had shipped him all over the country and he hadn't been sick a day.

And, in addition to all that, he'd displayed an all important ingredient in every race.

Class.

The only question about him was this: How good could he be?

There was something else that was positive, and it, too, goes into the mental toughness category. Not once had he been intimidated in a race. He had been outrun, but never intimidated.

There's an important point to re-emphasize here. One race doesn't make a horse, nor does one race break a horse. If you lose, as we did with Unbridled, it's just an indicator that you did something wrong; something happened over which no one had control or something just wasn't right with the horse. The same holds if the reverse is true. If you go out and "bury" a field on a given day, it doesn't mean that you have a world beater that will always be in the winner's circle. You hope you do, but it's possible the horse may fire like that only one in 10 times out.

It's only after you have run a horse at varying distances, against varying competition and over varying surfaces that you can begin to get a feel for what it will do on a race by race basis, and even then you will be wrong about as often as you are right.

I certainly wasn't discouraged with the way Unbridled ran in the Bluegrass. In fact, in an interview with ABC television before that race, I told them I didn't think Unbridled could beat Summer Squall over the Keeneland track, even if it were dry. The reason, I explained, was that Summer Squall was a speed horse with the added advantage of having tactical speed. Keeneland was a speed track and this set it up perfectly for him.

If I were to have tried to beat Summer Squall at his game in the Bluegrass, I would have had to take Unbridled out of his rhythm and run him near the leaders, something he had already told us he didn't like to do. My strategy for the Bluegrass was to let Unbridled run his race and hope Summer Squall didn't fire that day so we would have a chance to close on him down the lane.

As I have already pointed out, that didn't happen. Throw in a muddy track as an additional handicap for Unbridled and the race was set up to be run just the way it came about.

I was happy Unbridled finished third. It once again proved his class. If he had been just an average horse running under conditions he didn't like, he would have been last. Plus, I had witnessed the one thing I wanted to see. I saw that big bay sonofagun close on Summer Squall before he switched leads and backed off because of the slippery track. I now knew that if the Kentucky Derby happened to set up right for us, Unbridled had the ability to beat Summer Squall.

I was more concerned with how the horse came out of the race than whether he won it. Our goal was the Kentucky Derby. Don't misunderstand, we were trying to win the Bluegrass; we just didn't ask the horse for more than he was willing to give that day. It turned out to be good strategy because he came out of that race sharp and willing to go on.

That likely wouldn't have been the case if Craig had gone to the whip and really pressured him. If he had done that, we might have had a lemon that had been squeezed dry.

If you take an overtrained horse to the Derby you are

finished. You aren't going to win because you can't get the recovery you need in three weeks. I don't care if you have won five races in a row. You're history. That race will test every bone in your horse's body and he has to be at the top of his game. If he comes in there squeezed dry, he is going to run a bad race. It is just that simple.

Sunday, after the Bluegrass, we took Unbridled to the track and jogged him. He was relaxed and again cleaned up his food.

On Monday we walked him and then vanned to Churchill Downs where we again walked him and let him graze.

Any trainer who has run there will tell you that if you are to do well at Churchill Downs, you must have at least one good work over the track. I was of the opinion that it would require two good, strong, conditioning works, but I didn't want them to come too early. I wanted first to freshen the horse and make sure he was on his toes.

Things started going our way after we arrived at Churchill Downs. It had been a cold spring to this point and Unbridled had been using most of his energy to stay warm. He hadn't been gaining weight like I wanted him to do. He has the kind of build and metabolism rate that he could eat everything in sight and not get fat.

Shortly after arriving at Churchill, the weather changed. It got warm. Unbridled thrived on the warmth and the atmosphere. He just blossomed, putting on weight and getting more fit with each passing day. Something else made me feel confident.

Unbridled liked the Churchill Downs track.

It was about time for the first of his two scheduled works.

I told Craig Perret, who would ride Unbridled in the Derby, that I wanted a pretty sharp work. I said, I want it

146

sharp, but I don't want a "burn." (A burn is when you get the horse focused and on his toes every step of the way.) I wanted to save that for the final work before the Derby. I wanted him to breeze and finish galloping out strong to be sure Unbridled had gotten a good feel of the track.

The breeze was perfect.

It was a five-eighths mile work. They started at the three-quarter pole and did that first eighth in 13 and change (13-plus seconds). When they reached the five-eighths pole, the pace quickened and when they were at the quarter pole and Unbridled switched leads, Craig moved on him just enough to send him flying under the wire and then let him gallop out another eighth.

He was right where we wanted him. He finished the five-eighths in about 1:02 and had galloped out strongly, finishing six furlongs in 1:15. Craig had let Unbridled run, but hadn't asked him for extended speed. It was no black letter work that would send journalists scrambling for interviews, but it was perfect for the horse.

We had been at Churchill 12 days and Unbridled was moving toward a peak just the way we wanted.

Craig was grinning when he came off the track. "This colt is five lengths better than he was in the Bluegrass," he said.

Prior to the breeze with Craig, we had given Unbridled a mile at an extended gallop on the 10th day, finishing the second half in 52.2 and then galloped on another three-eighths a little slower. He came off the track on his toes that morning, so we knew he was asking for that first breeze.

The final tune-up breeze came on the morning of the 17th day. It was Monday and the race was Saturday. Again, Craig Perret was aboard and, again, it was a five-eighths mile breeze. As before, Craig started him at the three-quarter pole and did the first furlong to the five-eighths pole in 13 and change.

Also, as before, the pace quickened at the five-eighths pole. At the quarter pole, Unbridled was quietly asked for more run. He flashed under the wire in 1:00.2 and galloped out strong in 1:12.3.

This time when Craig came back to where I was standing, he was not only happy, but confident. "This horse is 10 lengths better than he was in the Bluegrass," he said. "We're going to win the Derby."

Everything was going right for Unbridled and that's what it takes to win the Kentucky Derby. You have to have all four traits functioning; you have to have a horse that shows class every time out and then you have to have things fall into place at the right time, both in training and in the race itself.

When all of that happens, you could win the Kentucky Derby.

There were some threats of rain before Derby Day and people who knew Unbridled were questioning what his chances would be if he had to run in the mud again. I didn't want rain either, but the worriers were missing a key point that I had finally realized. Unbridled didn't so much mind the wet track as he hated having it slippery. Churchill Downs is a track that can be wet and still not be slick. I felt he would run his race over that track, wet or dry.

The Derby is a day away. It's Friday. Time for me to use what I considered a small secret weapon with this particular horse. I had done it with him in nearly every race of his career, but had kept it secret from the press. A day prior to each of his races, instead of just galloping him for exercise, I would have the rider gallop about a mile and then quicken the pace to do the last half in 52 and change - a light breeze.

I kept that a secret race after race because if he would have thrown in a dull effort, the critics would have said it was because he'd been breezed the day before. But, remember, each horse is an individual and you must treat them accordingly. Unbridled could do a half in 52 and change and not really be extending himself. Instead of squeezing a drop from the lemon, I was merely adding to the potency of the contents.

Derby Day.

My great words of wisdom for Craig Perret in the paddock? There were none. Everything that could be said had been said and everything that could be done had been done with this horse. We had plotted the first small segment of his campaign to climax at Breeders' Cup. That didn't work when he bled. Then we regrouped and planned a whole new program, all of it aimed at bringing him to the Derby, fit and sharp. It worked. That doesn't make us geniuses. We had a solid schedule planned, the horse responded and a lot of things fell into place at the right time.

Unbridled was fit and ready to run for the roses on the first Saturday of May, 1990.

All I said to Craig Perret before the race was this: "You know the horse. Just ride your race. If a lane opens for us in the stretch, we'll win the Kentucky Derby."

More about the race itself later.

Let's give some attention to the pressures that are brought to bear on an owner and trainer when you have a "big" horse. What if that $40,000 yearling we've been discussing, blooms into a Derby contender? What is it like to own or train a horse like that?

First of all, there is one thing owner and trainer must guard against - the desire to win, win, win at all costs. Most people, when they have a good horse, don't want to be beaten. They love the exhilaration of coming under the wire first and can never get enough of that feeling.

As I've already said, one race doesn't make a horse and that must be kept constantly in mind, plus you simply can't

149

win them all. You are going to be campaigning this horse at a number of tracks on your way to the classics and each one will be different. If you have a horse that closes from off the pace like Unbridled, and you are at a fast track where speed is holding up that day, you are going to be hard-pressed to beat the speed horses. If your horse hates mud and you wind up running on a muddy track, the odds are against you. If you have a horse that loves to run on the front, but in a particular race, speed is "backing up", you are going to be lucky to hold on and win. One simply must accept the cards dealt as you move through your schedule and interpret what occurs, based on the conditions that existed that day.

The pressure to win, however, is so great that it causes trainers and owners to make more mistakes than any other single force.

Once you are at a track, such as Churchill Downs with the Derby coming up, you are in a fish bowl. Everything you do is scrutinized, evaluated and commented on. The way you train is compared to other successful trainers and so on.

I was given a bit of advice prior to the Derby that helped me and which I still value. This person said: "Carl, don't worry about all those other horses. Their owners and their trainers might mess them up. All I'd worry about is not messing up Unbridled."

Good advice. Let the other owners and trainers prepare their horses any way they want. You train and prepare the same way you have been doing. You know your horse. You understand his personality and his needs and you have adjusted to them. That is what brought you this far in the first place and what is going to give you success if you're fortunate enough to win a race like the Kentucky Derby.

Let your horse dictate your strategy. Take horses like Affirmed, Seattle Slew and Lost Code. They had a style of running that put them on the pace or in the lead throughout a

150

race. You don't try to change horses like that and try to make them come from way off the pace. You let them run their race. Then, you have a horse like Summer Squall who has tactical speed; a horse that loves to lay just off the pace and then explode. That's an ideal horse. Or, you have a horse like Unbridled that wants to come from out of it and close down the lane. A horse like that wants to be left alone until they are ready to make their one big run. Whatever it is your horse tells you he wants is what you let him do. And, you certainly don't change anything on the morning of a major race.

Leave them alone and let them run their race.

It is important at this point to state the obvious: there aren't many Seattle Slews, Unbridleds, Affirmeds, Summer Squalls or Lost Codes in the racing world. The majority of horses are of lesser ability, but you still must approach training and understanding of the horse in the same way.

A case in point. I had a little horse in training that loved to come from way off the pace. He was running in allowance races and making a strong bid down the lane each time, but consistently was coming up short.

The owner said I should be keeping the horse on the pace so he didn't have so much ground to make up. I tried to tell him this horse, mentally, was like Unbridled. He had no desire to mix it up in the early going, but would make a strong bid at the end.

The man said: "This horse is no Unbridled."

I replied: "True, but if you let me run him for $20,000 claiming instead of allowance, he would be."

If you're going to truly appreciate racing, you must learn to enjoy the horse for its ability, no matter what the level. If it's a classic horse, rejoice; if it isn't, run it at a level where it's competitive and appreciate the effort it'll give you.

There's another danger when you have the "big" horse. You start reading your press clippings and listening to your growing list of friends. It's amazing, by the way, how many friends you have when you're winning and on your way to the Derby. They are quick to tell you why you got beat in a certain race or what you did right when you win.

I've been training for 25 years and, as I've mentioned earlier, I've had little help in training the bad horses, but a lot of suggestions with the good ones.

As an owner, it's hard not to read the press clippings and to be affected by them. Don't let this kind of publicity influence you.

I can better illustrate my point with a story. When I was a young bull rider on the professional rodeo circuit, I was riding good. Real good. A reporter interviewed me and then wrote a glowing story, talking about how good I was and how I might be the next World Champion.

It got me all excited and my ego inflated. I took the story to an old friend who was like a second father to me. "Read it," I told him. "They think I'm pretty great."

He read the story all the way through and then laid down the paper and looked me in the eye. "There's only one problem with the article, Carl, them bulls can't read."

Well, racehorses can't read either. They measure themselves against each other and that's when and where class is expressed. They have no idea what some writer is saying they can or cannot do. Unbridled probably never would have won the Derby if he could read. He would have said, "Oh, I'm only fifth or sixth at best in this race. There's no way I can win."

The person giving you all this free advice, more often than not, is just trying to say what he or she thinks you want to hear. They just want to be your friend while you have the big horse so they can bask in your glory. That same person may not remember your name when you hit one of the inevitable lows that comes to us all if we stay in this business long enough.

If that adviser wants to be a trainer and give advice, he can buy a trainer's license. And, if he wants to be an owner, he can buy a horse.

I stand on a comment I made about the Derby, and you can apply it to any "big" horse: "The Kentucky Derby is one of the greatest events you can ever be part of, but if you try to become the event, it will destroy you."

Winning the Derby is like becoming Miss America for a year. Members of the press accompany Carl Nafzger on the backside after Unbridled's Derby win.

Photo by Dan Johnson

Winning the Kentucky Derby is something like becoming Miss America for a year. Suddenly, you are transformed in the minds of the public into something that you aren't. Now, you know everything there is to know about horses, when in fact, you know nothing more than you did the day of the race. Now, your horse isn't just a racehorse; its an illusion. The fact is, that "illusion" could bow a tendon tomorrow.

When you win a race like the Derby, you become a "Greek God", but remember, next year there's going to be another Greek God.

Chapter 12

Taking an Alternate Route

We have taken a look at the route to follow for a young colt or filly that has talent and can handle training and racing pressure. But, what about the other type that we mentioned earlier; the horse that has pedigree, appears to be talented, but mentally can't handle the stress of training and racing? The traits of soundness, ability and a good immune system all are present, but the youngster simply can't handle the stress of training and racing.

Let's take a look at some alternate routes, including turf racing.

First, this young prospect should be returned to the farm to alleviate the on-track stress and to give it a chance to mature and develop both mentally and physically.

I should caution at this point that the rate of success with horses of this type is not high. If you have a horse that can't handle training and racing stress as a two-year-old, you have only about a 20 percent chance that it will handle stress as a three-year-old. However, if it's a good colt or filly that has the other three traits in line, we must give it an additional opportunity.

The first thing to be done is to simply turn the horse out for a time. Just let them be a horse. Let them roam in a paddock or pasture all day or even day and night. Whatever it takes to completely change the environment so that the horse is removed from the stress of training and racing.

If it's a colt, we should give consideration to turning it

into a gelding. Remember, we bought this horse to be a racehorse, not a breeding stallion. We should give it every chance to become a successful runner, but it doesn't have the ability, there are a number of other avenues open for its future, such as jumping, eventing, dressage, trail riding and other equestrian activities. However, most of those options aren't open for stallions.

Anytime a young colt shows undue stud-like tendencies, such as nervousness, agitation when other horses go by, sweaty just from going to the track, getting nippy with people in the stall - bite and flight where he snaps at you and then moves quickly away - it's time for him to be gelded. I have also found that some colts will get off balance physically as they develop as unaltered males. Some will get heavy in the front end and cresty in the neck, thus bringing an imbalance to their bodies because they'll be traveling too heavily on their front ends.

Some colts turn rank and mean as they develop. I have had only a few of them, but they're out there, believe me. Mean colts should be gelded without a second thought as a protection for the people handling them.

Still others suffer pain from their testicles when running and won't give you their best effort until gelded.

To summarize, if you geld a colt you not only open wider the door to potential racing success but, if that doesn't happen, you have turned him into a horse that is marketable in another discipline. There just simply is no future for a young Thoroughbred stallion that can't run.

I know it is the dream of many racehorse owners to not only have a runner that can win the Derby, but to also have a stallion that is syndicated for millions of dollars. That happens, but it's rare. You have to have everything working just right - pedigree and a highly successful track record.

I remember one good horse we had that earned about a

million dollars. He had a decent pedigree, good speed and a solid track record. We put him at stud and he bred probably 25 mares at $2,500 each that first year. I point this out to emphasize that new owners should not be blinded by dreams of having their colt become the next Northern Dancer where mare owners are standing in line.

Back to the farm.

I recommend that the young horse be turned out no less than two months and perhaps three. Rear shoes will be pulled and if the horse is wearing toe grabs in front, we'll replace them with keg shoes that have no grabs. When the horse gets feeling frisky and playful in the paddock, we don't want it injuring itself by grabbing a quarter (striking the buttress of a front heel with the shod toe of a rear foot).

Generally, the young horse will be turned into the round pen for about four days to sort of wind down from race training and get acclimated to new surroundings. When it appears comfortable and relaxed, it will be turned into a paddock, generally by itself, especially if it's a colt. Fillies sometimes are turned out in groups.

I prefer to have this youngster left outside 24 hours a day with a run-in shelter available in the paddock or pasture so it can get out of the sun or rain. At this point, I don't want the horse to have any stress other than coping with the weather.

While the horse is being let down, I want it to have unlimited exercise on its own terms in the paddock, access to salt and minerals and good daily nourishment. There is one thing I do not want. I do not want this horse to gain weight. Its metabolism will change and it will lose some of its muscle tone, but by properly regulating the diet, we can prevent the horse from putting on harmful layers of fat.

If the horse becomes fat, we have compounded our problem when it's time to once again put it into race training. With an obese horse, we'll have to spend a lot of time replacing fat with muscle before we have an opportunity to learn whether it benefited from its layoff. And while we're doing this, we put the horse at additional risk of injury because it is carrying a heavier burden on muscles, tendons and ligaments that are not in the hardened condition they were when the horse left the track.

The good news is that modern-day equine nutrition is such that a ration can easily be designed to keep a horse in the bloom of good health, without adding excess weight, even when it's being turned out.

When that young horse comes back into training you should be able to see definition of withers and a shading of ribs.

After 30 to 60 days at the lay-up farm, the horse will be taken to a training farm. Rarely will you want it to be brought back to the track at this point because the horse, first of all, most likely won't be ready yet to face the stress of training on the track and, secondly, it generally is more economical to bring the horse back into condition at a training farm rather than at the track.

We will want the young horse to remain at the training farm for 30 to 45 days, where it will be doing a lot of jogging and galloping to get its muscles and bones strengthened once again. At the end of that time frame, the horse will be returned to the track.

When the horse arrives back on the track, we will want to increase the amount of energy it gets from the feed ration. When the colt or filly was at the lay-up farm, it was on a low energy ration. When it went to the training farm, the energy level was raised. Now, that it's back at the track, that energy level will be raised even more, but we must be careful to do it gradually. We will increase the energy level in line with increasing demands of the training regimen. We will talk more about feeding later.

Horses that are turned out and then brought back into

training generally regain fitness quickly since they never completely lose their muscle tone. In addition, if they have had a race or two under their belts as two-year-olds, they know why they are at the track. We won't have to go through the same acclimating process we did when they were two.

The big question is whether the layoff did the horse any good. Was it just not mature enough early in its two-year-old year to handle the stress, or do we have a horse that never will be able to cope with race track pressures?

The morning after the horse arrives at the track, we will just hand walk it to get it used to being on the shedrow again. We might even do this for two days and then we will begin jogging and galloping with our first stride breeze of a half mile in 52 or 53 seconds coming about 10 days after arrival. This shouldn't produce undue stress because the horse will already have had a couple stride breezes at the training farm.

After being returned to the track, we will be studying the horse closely on an almost hour by hour basis. Is it cleaning up its feed? Does it seem relaxed in the stall? Is it relaxed when going to the track or is it jittery and sweaty?

We are going to know how to read this horse quickly because of our past experience with it. If it handles going to the track, jogging, galloping and breezing without demonstrating undue stress, we can begin thinking about racing in approximately 60 days.

The approach in determining the correct training schedule for this horse will be he same as when it was started. We will observe, learn and adjust to its needs. If it needs lots of long gallops, that's what it will get. If it needs frequent breezes, that's what we will do. As before, the needs of the horse will dictate our training.

One thing I should discuss here is timing, relative to bringing the horse back into training. By following the above scenario, we'll have laid the young prospect off during the summer months of its two-year-old year and brought it back into training in the fall which will have it ready for winter racing.

We might want to alter this schedule because winter racing is getting tougher and tougher. There are fewer races available to meet the demands we might have for a young, developing colt or filly. In addition, many of the horses running in the winter meets are proven, seasoned campaigners; pretty rugged company for a young horse that was having stress problems as a two-year-old that spring.

Winter meets in the south are very condensed because of the large number of horses that will be running in places like Gulfstream, Santa Anita, or Oaklawn Park. An option might be to take the young prospect to a northern track, but that isn't usually a good idea because you are at the mercy of the weather. There will be days when cold or snow will make it impossible to train. Veteran runners can handle this type of disruptive schedule, but it isn't recommended for a three-year-old that didn't fare well in training at age two. You will have trouble getting the horse fit and it will be difficult to establish an appropriate training schedule. You just simply can't get a rhythm established under these on again, off again cold weather conditions.

What we might want to do is lay the horse off for a longer period, perhaps until winter, then bring it back and have it fit and poised for the spring and summer campaigns as a three-year-old when many more racing opportunities will be available. During the spring and summer we will be better able to spot our young prospect in races where it will have a chance to do well and, hopefully, continue to develop satisfactorily.

So where are we at this point with our theoretical $40,000 purchase? We have spent another $25,000 in training and development costs, so our investment at this point is

160

$65,000. Because of what happened with this young horse as a two-year-old, we have faced the fact that we don't have a world beater. Our goals become less ambitious. Instead of winning the Derby, we're going to attempt to recoup our $65,000 investment.

Patience.

This is not the time to rush off pell-mell and look for a quick fix or fast sale, providing the horse has demonstrated ability. If we have decided the horse is worth giving a second chance, then we truly must provide it and under the correct conditions.

Let us assume the horse is demonstrating that all of the traits, except its capability to handle stress as a two-year-old, are in place. The time frame we're looking at to bring a horse back, get it racing and, hopefully, either be winning races or getting it sold, encompasses about five months.

Let us assume that when this horse comes back to the track, it exhibits all the positive signs. The feed tub is cleaned up every day, it goes to the track in relaxed, but workmanlike fashion, it remains sound, its immune system is functioning beautifully and the horse shows even more ability than we observed as a two-year-old. Some horses are as good as they are ever going to be at two, but others need maturity to blossom.

The big test comes about 60 days after returning to the track when we enter the horse in its first race as a three-year-old. We will pick a race where we believe it can be competitive. Our expectations in that first race will be much the same as when the horse got its first start as a two-year-old. If it leaves the gate in the lead, but gets passed in the stretch, we won't worry, providing the horse comes back to the barn calm and relaxed, cleans up its feed and remains relaxed after the race.

We will be even happier if it starts in the middle of the pack or near the rear and then is passing horses in the stretch.

Again, under this scenario, we won't worry about where the horse finishes, providing that it was gaining ground and running strong at the finish.

If the horse comes back from its first outing after finishing second, third or fourth, cleans up its feed and shows no sign of stress, you, the owner, and the trainer can congratulate yourselves. You made a good decision. You have a three-year-old runner with a bright future.

If, however, the horse comes back nervous and upset, refusing to eat, we know we made a mistake. We are now dealing with a horse where the odds are mounting on the side of failure instead of success. We might want to give it one more race in the same kind of company, but if the stress signs appear again, it is time to do what we now wish we had done as a two-year-old - drop the horse in value in a claiming race and accept our losses.

What about the horse that's in between? The one that doesn't quite come back, but definitely isn't a washout?

This type of horse can be frustrating, to say the least. Usually, it's a horse that has ability, but something always gets in the way of success.

It's time for some serious observation and adjustments.

If, for example, we are running this horse at six furlongs and it isn't handling it, perhaps we should be thinking about longer races. Maybe this horse would run well on turf. There are horses that run very poorly on dirt, but love the grass.

Running on the grass can become an option, but the problem with turf racing, particularly in the Midwest, is there aren't many races offered. If you have a turf horse, you will be lucky to get it in one race per month. Then, there are special conditions for entering a turf race as tracks attempt to keep the entries at a manageable level.

While I never buy a horse for turf racing and do not train them for turf, it can be a positive option for horses that show ability, but don't run well on dirt.

A case in point is a filly we had in training that was an "in between" prospect that eventually blossomed on the grass.

The filly started on the dirt as a two-year-old and did well, but then developed some foot problems. We turned her out about six months to grow additional hoof and then brought her back. She was training very well and within a couple months was fit and appeared eager to run.

In her first race as a three-year-old, I told the jockey to just go ahead and let her run out of the gate. I thought she could win anywhere. This filly ran about half a mile and looked awesome. Then, she just hung it up. She quit running. I thought it had to be a fluke because she was training so beautifully.

We ran her again. Same thing. After about half a mile, she just quit.

She was telling us she didn't like what we were asking her to do.

Time to adjust.

She was a filly with a good pedigree, was sound, had a good immune system and demonstrated ability at every training session. We decided she was worth an extended effort to find her niche. We did run her back in a sprint race again, only this time I had the jockey keep her off the pace. There was improvement, but she still wasn't close to the winner at the wire.

Next I ran her a mile and a sixteenth, thinking she needed additional distance. It was frustrating. She was only about three lengths off the lead at the three-eighths pole (three-eighths of a mile from the finish line) when she stopped again. Just when she was to put in a big move, she did the opposite. She stopped.

After this race about everybody was losing faith in her, including the owner. I insisted that she had a ton of talent and

163

a good mind; we just hadn't found what suited her yet.

I put her back in a sprint race and had the jockey relax her. She was dead last until the head of the stretch. When he asked her to run, she took off, passing four or five horses, though still finishing out of the money.

The owners remained discouraged, but I was elated. She had proven she could and would run, though I knew we still hadn't found what suited her best. Her pedigree revealed that she was bred for the turf. This, I had thought all along, would be her strong suit, but I felt that I had to get her mind focused on running an entire race on dirt before trying her on turf.

By now we were in the midst of the winter meet at Gulfstream Park, not a good place to be developing a filly that has moved into her four-year-old year. The owners wanted to take her out of training and breed her, but agreed to give me a chance to try her on turf before doing so.

We moved to Keeneland in the spring and the filly continued training very well. I ran her in a sprint race on dirt again and once more had the jockey keep her off the pace. This time she came running and finished second.

Great.

I didn't let myself celebrate because one good race doesn't make a racehorse and she'd had some bad ones along the way. I figured she would have to have three good races in a row to prove that she was the kind of runner I had been claiming she could be.

We moved to Churchill Downs.

We followed the same strategy with her first sprint race on dirt there and she finished second again, only this time she was closing on the leader.

I'm feeling good.

We came back with her a third time at Churchill. Same strategy. Keep her off the pace and then let her close. Third this time, but she's flying down the home stretch. She's proven she can and will run.

I felt the time had come to try her on turf around two turns, but there didn't appear to be any coming up that would fit her needs in the near future.

There were plenty of dirt races around two turns, but she had already demonstrated that she didn't like dirt at a distance.

Time to be patient.

I wouldn't run her until a turf race opened. Luckily, they split a condition race for which this filly was eligible and she was in. The race was a mile and an eighth on the grass. Now, we were going to find out if the strategy of keeping her off the pace and then letting her run would work on the turf and around two turns.

I told the jockey to just get her to relax in the early going; to be dead last. I told him not to worry if he was a length behind the last place horse going down the back stretch; that he should sit tight and wait. Don't move on this filly, I told him, until you have a quarter of a mile to go. He did exactly as he was told and didn't ask her to run until the head of the stretch. When he did, she started moving between and past horses, gaining ground with every stride. She didn't win, but that race revealed that she'd found her niche.

Now, we had two things in our favor, in addition to her four traits of ability, soundness, good mental attitude and an excellent immune system; she loved the grass and she wanted to come from off the pace. She went on to become a successful turf horse.

I mention her because she is an example of that in between horse that can be so frustrating to owner and trainer alike. She didn't go out there and win as a three-year-old, but she continued to demonstrate all of the necessary traits to be successful and, after we'd made all the necessary adjustments, she became both happy and successful.

Again, I don't really advise buying and training horses for turf racing because there simply aren't enough turf races in America to make it worthwhile. However, in the case of this filly, the turf was just what she wanted and needed. It proved to be the correct antidote for an in between horse.

To me the turf remains an alternative, rather than a focal point when I'm training young prospects.

I have found that horses with high action often will perform better on turf than dirt and horses that tend to have rear end problems seem to do better on the turf, perhaps because there is less slippage of the rear feet.

Some trainers feel they must train on the turf in order to get horses ready to run on it. I don't find that to be the case. Coolawin is a case in point. A successful dirt horse, she won her first stakes race, a Grade III, on the turf and never had worked over it before. She loved it.

It takes a more fit horse to run on the turf, generally speaking. Sometimes a turf race can tighten a horse up for a dirt race. I love to run a horse on the turf and then, for its next out, put it in a seven furlong race on dirt. The turf race will have honed those muscles to an even sharper edge.

Let's leave our not so good and in between prospects and go back to our theoretical young colt or filly that turned out well. How are we going to train it for its three and four-year-old campaigns? The best way for me to discuss this is to once again use Unbridled as an example. He was a success at both three and four years of age as well as at two.

Time to pick up on him again as we discuss campaigning a successful three-year-old through summer and into the fall.

Chapter 13

Three-Year-Old Campaign

The Derby was over.

Wanda and I needed a break, so we flew to Arizona to be alone and come to grips with everything that was happening in our lives. We knew things would never be quite the same, but we also knew that down inside, we were still Carl and Wanda Nafzger, two very fortunate people to have a horse like Unbridled come along at this point in our lives.

We knew that with two of the Triple Crown races ahead of us, there would be unrelenting media pressure. No longer could we just quietly lead Unbridled into the saddling paddock. He wasn't just Unbridled anymore. He was the Derby winner.

There was, we decided, one thing we could do to cope with all of the attention. We could refuse to let it change us as individuals. We would enjoy this heady ride at the top, but would not let it consume us.

Fortified with that resolve, we headed back into the spotlight.

There would be no Triple Crown for Unbridled.

He came out of the Derby in great shape, so all of his traits for success were in order. He was mentally attuned, sound, healthy and still full of run. We kept him at Churchill Downs and then flew into Baltimore for the Preakness.

We had a great time and it was a good race. Unbridled was forced to make his move a little earlier than we wanted in order to get into contention and as a result didn't have his patented big punch down the lane. He finished second to Summer Squall.

Let the record show that those two horses ran the last three-sixteenths of a mile as fast as its ever been run in the Preakness.

Next came the Belmont.

There are no two ways about it. I trained the horse completely wrong for the Belmont. Remember, what I said earlier? That Unbridled didn't make mistakes? Jockeys did, owners did and trainers did, but not Unbridled.

Well, the Belmont was my mistake. We went in on three-quarter works that were too fast. I had too much speed in the horse for this type of race. We didn't need that much speed. We needed more muscle and strengthened ligaments and tendons for endurance on that looser, sandier track. The best human analogy I can come up with is the person who trains on hard dirt and then must run his race on a sandy beach. It's a plenty safe surface, but it takes a different set of muscles.

As far as speed is concerned, I trained too much like I did for the Derby and the Preakness. I trained for speed when he didn't need speed in this particular race. Instead of working five eighths of a mile in fractions of 12 and change or 13.1 seconds for each eighth, I should have been working him a mile at a slower pace and just let him run the last quarter

I also freshened Unbridled too much. I was thinking he needed more of a break from serious training than he did. I should have just kept on with him as we had before the Derby and the Preakness because he was getting better and better. Instead, we backed off and this turned out to be wrong.

Unbridled finished fourth in the Belmont and it was the most disappointing race with which I had ever been involved. That fourth came as a result of his training, not his class. If he hadn't been such a class horse, he would have finished farther back than he did.

I was dejected. Not because we lost, but because the horse had run his heart out for me and I hadn't brought him into the race prepared to win the Belmont. Basically, he was trained to run a mile and one-eighth and the Belmont is a mile and one-half.

The only positive I could find at that moment was that at least I knew what I had done wrong. I would never make those mistakes with him again.

The next morning I had to face the press. Everybody wanted to know what my plans were for Unbridled.

I told them my only immediate plans were to freshen the horse and then begin preparing him for a campaign that would culminate with the Breeders' Cup Classic.

"I will be back and Unbridled will win the Breeders' Cup Classic here at Belmont Park this fall," I told them and I meant it. I also meant what I said next, though I didn't realize at the time how tough it would be to stay the planned course: "Nothing counts between now and the Classic."

We left New York and went to Arlington Park in Chicago. Now, I had an opportunity to truly let every on the Unbridled team take a break from the frenetic pace we'd been maintaining.

As with everything else, Unbridled took things in stride. He enjoyed his rest, but when we headed back for some serious training, he was ready and eager.

For his first race after the Belmont, I opted for an allowance race at seven-eighths of a mile at Arlington. I didn't want something as tough as a stakes race after the Belmont. I wanted a race where we wouldn't have to demand as much from him in this, his first step along the road back to Belmont Park in the Breeders' Cup Classic.

It was now late summer.

The problem was finding such a race. Then good

fortune came our way. An allowance race for which he was qualified was offered at Arlington at exactly the time I felt Unbridled was in need of some competition.

Earlie Fires was the jockey and he rode a great race. Unbridled was brilliant. When Earlie asked him for run, he just exploded and won it going away by seven lengths or more.

I had kept my next move with him a secret from everyone except his owners, the Genters. I had decided Unbridled would benefit from a mile and one-quarter race on the turf, even though he had never before trained or raced on turf.

We worked him on the turf at Arlington and, though it didn't seem to be his choice of surfaces, he handled it well. My logic was this. The horse had just run a brilliant speed race on the dirt. What he needed next was a longer race over a more giving surface that would tighten his muscles, especially in the rear end and stifles.

Earlie Fires was again the jockey. Before the race I told him: "Earlie, you sit on this horse and don't let him make a move until the half-mile pole. I want him last, seven or eight lengths off the pace, but I want a hard last half mile on him. I want everything out of this horse in that last half mile that he has to give."

I knew that asking him to run at the half mile pole was earlier than he'd normally give his big kick, but remember, I'm preparing this horse for the Breeders' Cup classic, not for a career on the turf. We needed a hard last half mile on the turf, which puts additional stress on certain muscles that aren't called into the same kind of play on the dirt. I wanted to tighten those muscles for the Belmont Park sand.

I wanted him to run that first three-quarters of a mile like a good strong gallop that he could do easily in 12 and change or 13 for each eighth.

Earlie rode him just the way I asked and when

Unbridled was asked to run, he did and he got the lead. However, the distance and the surface did get to him and he tired in the stretch. A nice little grass horse we had called Super Abound had been laying dead last because his jockey was under instructions to just ride the race as it shaped up. Randy Romero was riding Super Abound and he made his move on the turn for home, caught Unbridled in the stretch and beat him.

Unbridled was one tired sonofagun when he came out of that race, but I'd gotten exactly what I wanted - an excellent conditioning effort.

It wasn't seen that way by the press. They really came down on me. What on earth are you doing, running this horse on the grass? they wanted to know.

All I told them was that it was what I wanted to do at the time. I didn't tell them my reasoning because I figured if I did, they'd just tell the rest of the world how dumb I was. That's the way it is when you have the "big" horse. When you get beat, everyone in the world is ready to step up and tell you what you did wrong. When you win they love you.

I had explained my reasoning to the owners and they were comfortable with it. I assured them Unbridled would be fit and ready for the Breeders' Cup Classic and, as I had said earlier, nothing in between that and the Classic really mattered. That was our goal and we stayed focused on it.

Now we faced the question of where to go next. Both Unbridled and Home At Last were nominated for the Super Derby in Louisiana Downs. We had definitely decided to take Home At Last, but hadn't really planned to run Unbridled there.

Unbridled came out of the turf race in great shape and we needed to find another race for him. Basically, our options at this point were to run him in the Meadowlands Cup or go to the Super Derby. Unbridled was shaping up to be fit and ready

171

for another race by Super Derby time and the Meadowlands Cup was three weeks later.

We decided to take both horses - Unbridled and Home At Last - to the Super Derby in Louisiana. I talked to the owner of Home At Last to make certain he had no objections. He didn't. We all knew that Home At Last was as fit as he had ever been and was ready to run a strong race.

So was Unbridled.

There was a class field entered for the Super Derby. Among them was Summer Squall. It was a class race and a test by fire no matter how you looked at it.

Summer Squall got sick before the race and was scratched. The press asked me who I thought had the class speed now that Summer Squall was out of the race. Without Summer Squall, I replied, the class speed belonged to Home At Last.

They scoffed at that.

Jose Velez was on Unbridled for the race and Jerry Bailey was riding Home At Last. As the race unfolded, Unbridled was right where I wanted him, about seven or eight lengths out of it. At the half-mile pole, he indicated he wanted to run and Jose let him go.

Well, when he started passing horses, the other jockeys also asked for run because they knew he could blow right by them down the stretch if they didn't. There was only one jockey who didn't ask his horse to run at this point. Jerry Bailey on Home At Last. He just sat quiet and cool while the field bunched around him. With everybody bunching up like that, Unbridled was forced to go five wide on the turn to get around them. He passed them all and now, he's in the stretch, but his big kick is fading.

With three-sixteenths of a mile to go, Home At Last˙ switched leads and Jerry Bailey asked him to run. He maintained his lead and won the race with Unbridled finishing second. Despite starting his speed spurt early and being forced five wide on the turn, the big bay had still finished second in that field of class horses.

The press saw it differently and really came down on me hard the next day. Getting beat in the Super Derby was an indication that Unbridled wasn't all that great, they said. He was falling apart.

I was angry and frustrated. Falling apart? A horse that had won a sprint race on dirt going away, finished second in his first ever turf race and now had finished second in a field of class horses? Falling apart? At this point in his career, Home At Last had never finished worse than third and had run a great race to win. Unbridled falling apart? Not to my way of thinking.

He was right on schedule.

Of course, I did not share with the critical press my overall plan for conditioning and tightening for the Classic.

My phone rang off the wall. To redeem himself, I was told, Unbridled would have to run in the Meadowlands Cup against Summer Squall and a tough field. If he didn't do that and win, they argued, I might as well forget the Classic and any hope of Unbridled being named Three-Year-Old Champion in the Eclipse Awards.

It was about this time that I decided an unlisted phone number was a good idea.

I simply didn't answer the critics.

Unbridled came out of the Super Derby a tired horse, but it wasn't the same kind of exhaustion he had shown after the Belmont. Quite the contrary. He was simply race tired, or "empty," and needed to freshen up or, as we say in racing, "fill his tank" again. He bounced back stronger, more focused and more eager to train.

It was five and one-half weeks before the Breeders' Cup and I had a horse that was fit and ready. Everything we had

173

done with him thus far had worked exactly as I'd hoped. The seven-eighths allowance race on dirt had allowed him to flash his speed, the turf race had tightened those rear end muscles and the Super Derby had forced him to give a maximum effort.

Remember, of course, that the fitness didn't come just from the races in which he'd been entered. We were training him differently, with longer gallops, plus gallops on the turf when possible. We weren't training for speed, we were planning and working to get a horse at the top of his game on a sandy track in the richest race of the year, the $3 million Classic. This training approach, plus the three races, gave us a hardened and eager racehorse.

What should we do next?

We decided to bypass the Meadowlands Cup and go directly to the Breeders' Cup Classic.

Unbridled was fit and ready. He didn't need another race. We now backed off a bit in our training regimen to freshen him and then continued building him toward a peak on Breeders' Cup Day.

I must at this point mention something that smacks of the unsavory in horse racing.

The rumor mill.

When I decided against running Unbridled in the Meadowlands Cup, the rumors started to fly. The most persistent one was that Unbridled was sore. Denying it did little good.

The rumors worsened. Now they were saying that the horse shouldn't be running in the Breeders' Cup, that the only reason I insisted on doing so was to feed my ego.

There was nothing to do, but turn a deaf ear.

We elected to stay at Keeneland to prepare for the Classic. Unbridled trained magnificently and now I had to decide what kind of works to put into him as race day approached. I chose a light half mile in 52 seconds, another

174

half in 49 seconds, three-quarters in 1:14 and change, all at Keeneland.

We shipped to Belmont Park several days before the Classic and worked him three-quarters of a mile there in 1:13 and change.

Again, the critics looked at us and shook their heads. The favorites in the Classic were working three-quarters in 1:11.1 and 1:12.1. We were dawdling by comparison.

I refused to budge from our approach. To make it easier on myself, I refused to read a newspaper or look at a racing form for about two weeks before the race. I kept remembering the advice I had received before the Derby. Let the other trainers and owners do what they will with their horses, you just make sure you don't screw up with yours.

Our approach was unorthodox, but it was a result of what we've been talking about all along. Knowing your horse and adjusting to its needs. Unbridled had let me know that I made a mistake in preparing him for the Belmont. I wasn't going to be wrong twice, no matter what the critics said. I knew my horse and I knew what was best for him.

This wasn't Churchill Downs and the Kentucky Derby. This was Belmont and the Breeders' Cup. A different track surface and a different race. Because the tracks and the races weren't the same, neither was the preparation for them.

In my heart, I knew Unbridled was fit and ready.

Then came the draw for post position.

The prevailing opinion was that no one could win the Breeders' Cup Classic if you drew from the eighth hole out. You had to draw in the inside seven if you were to have a chance.

We drew number 14. As far out as you could possibly get because there were 14 horses in the field.

The press really wrote him off then.

That's horse racing. You accept what happens and go

on from there.

Pat Day was to be aboard Unbridled again.

Quite frankly, I wasn't concerned about post position and when Pat and I talked I said so. "I don't see it as any kind of a disadvantage," I said, "because we don't want any part of the front end in the early going anyway."

Pat agreed.

Remember the rumors I was talking about? On the morning of Breeders' Cup, we'd gone to the track and then returned to the hotel to freshen up. The phone rang. It was Joe Hirsch from the Racing Form.

"How's Unbridled," he asked.

"Fine," I said.

"No problems?"

"No problems, Joe, I really feel confident."

"Okay," he said, "just wishing you luck."

That was strange. Joe Hirsch calling me on race day morning just to ask about the horse and wish us good luck.

We arrived at Belmont, checked in at the barn and headed to the races. Just as we got to the grandstand before the first race, some press members said, "Sorry to hear about Unbridled."

"Hear what?" I asked, dumbfounded.

"That he's sore and you've scratched him."

"He's not sore and I didn't scratch him," I said.

Now I knew why Joe had called. He, too, had heard the "scratch" rumor and was calling to check it out.

A bit shaken by this turn of events, I called the stewards to double check if there was something I didn't know. After all, I was the only one who could scratch the horse unless the track veterinarian had ruled him unsound.

"No," they said, "he's still entered for the Classic."

Rumors.

Sometimes benign. Sometimes vicious. If you're going

to be in racing and have success, you will not only have to learn to handle the pressures of the media and the fish bowl attention, but you also have to learn to cope with rumors which you are powerless to control or stop.

Our strategy for the Breeders' Cup Classic was basic. "I'm not going to tell you how to ride this race, Pat," I said. "All I'm going to say is that if you're within about seven lengths of

Unbridled wins the Breeders' Cup Classic
Photo by Dan Johnson

the lead at the quarter-pole and haven't used him hard to get there, you'll win this horse race if a lane opens."

You can check the video. At the quarter-pole, Unbridled was just about exactly seven lengths from the lead. He was running about ninth at that point. The other horses had already made their moves, but Unbridled hadn't.

A lane opened.

I saw Pat send him through that bunch without having to veer or change course.

I looked at Wanda. "We're going to win the Breeders' Cup Classic," I said.

By now he's four lengths from the lead and has a clear path to the wire. The rest is history. He just exploded in those final strides and won it by a length.

A triumphant Pat Day makes his way through the crowd of fans after Unbridled's win in the Breeders' Cup Classic.

Photo by Dan Johnson

We were heroes again.

But, here's a lesson to be learned and remembered.

Here I was, sending a horse to the track that had not had a race in five and one-half weeks, a horse that had drawn the 14th post position and a horse that was rumored to be dead lame and was being run only to feed my ego.

If we had finished in the back of the pack, I would have been the focal point of criticism as a trainer who didn't care about his horse and ran him even though he was sore.

Sometimes, in this business, the line between what's perceived by the press and public as hero or villain is as close as a photo finish.

When you are winning everyone loves you and is your friend. When the same horse loses, many of the same people become your critics and your enemies. I finally had my shot at the press after the Classic. Which victory with Unbridled was greatest, I was asked. The Derby or the Classic?

If I pick one or the other, I'm going to get clobbered by somebody, I think.

So I said, "Well, you have to think of the historic value of the Kentucky Derby. To win it was a great honor. But, the most satisfying victory was the Breeders' Cup Classic."

Nobody printed that because I added one more sentence.

"It was the most satisfying because it shut up every one of you-all."

I had a short interview that day.

That crack might have cost Unbridled Horse of The Year honors because it sure offended some members of the press. However, some who I consider to be the more responsible representatives of the media, praised me for telling it like it was.

I don't mean to paint a grim picture here for owners and future owners, but dealing with a sometimes hostile press is part of the overall scenario and you have to be prepared to cope with it when you are successful and lucky enough to have the "big" horse come your way.

For us, the three-year-old campaign was over. Unbridled still was demonstrating that all four necessary traits were in fine order. He was in excellent spirits mentally; he was sound; he still had not been sick a day and, of course, we didn't

179

have to wonder about his ability.

We decided he should have some time off and then be campaigned as a four-year-old.

That brings us to another subject, campaigning the older horse.

Chapter 14

Campaigning the Older Horse

Training and racing an older horse - one that's four or over - is, generally speaking, less trying than preparing a two or three-year-old for competition.

The reason is basic. By the time a horse is in its four-year-old year on the track, there should be few surprises as to temperament, soundness, immune system and ability.

However, sometimes strange things happen with ability as a horse gets older. A three-year-old stakes winner, for example, doesn't always graduate into being a four and older stakes winner. The older campaigners that become stakes winner are truly old war horses and they know all the tricks involved in winning a race. It's a similar situation to a young pro in the National Football League going up against a six or eight-year veteran. The younger pro might be a little quicker and more athletic, but the old pro knows all the right moves.

In a crucial game, a young pro lineman might be having that older guy for lunch throughout the game and be thinking, "Hey, there's nothing to this guy who's supposed to be a legend. I can block him out of every play." But just let it get down to fourth and goal and all of a sudden that old veteran is blowing past the young guy and spilling the runner in the backfield for a five-yard loss. The young guy can only shake his head and wonder what happened.

That's the way it is with the veteran racehorse who has a successful graduation from the three-year-old ranks to four and older. He simply knows how to win races when the chips are down.

The veteran is an easier horse to train because you know what he likes and what he doesn't like and you should have learned what type of competition he can handle, what sort of track he runs best on and how many works, gallops and jogs he needs between races. Above all, you should understand what type of pattern he's set for himself when running a race.

A good example of what I'm talking about is a horse we had in the stable called Hold Old Blue. If a race shaped up just right for Hold Old Blue, he was a world beater. If it didn't, he just kind of galloped along with the also rans. If he decided on a given day that this wasn't his race to win, the jockey might just as well put the whip away and go along for the ride.

When Hold Old Blue left the gate, he would always leave running. How he finished depended on what the leaders did. If the speed held up that day, Hold Old Blue would just cruise along and never extend himself. However, if the leaders began to weaken at about the quarter pole, Hold Old Blue would sense it and just take off and go flying by everybody.

Regardless of what happened, win or lose, however, Hold Old Blue would go back to his stall after the race, totally relaxed. He would clean up his food and show nary a sign of stress. The next day he'd be ready to go to the track for a jog or gallop.

I trained a horse from Argentina named Joel, that was similar. Once we figured out how he wanted to run a race, we just stayed out of his way and let him do it. He came to the stable in Minnesota. He had some seconds and thirds, but he also had some terrible races. He acted in those bad races like he simply didn't want to run. I watched a bunch of videos of his earlier races and made a couple decisions. First, I took the blinkers off, and, second, told the jockey in the horse's first race for our stable to just sit on him and see what happened. We had to find out what he wanted to do and what he didn't want to do.

As it turned out, getting rid of the blinkers was a helpful step. However, the real change came when the horse found out he was being allowed to be as far off the pace as he desired and then could come running at the end. This was the way he wanted to run and once he was allowed to do it his way, it became his distinctive pattern and he was a winner.

What made him such a good racehorse running that style of race, we discovered, was his ability to clock the field and know exactly when to make his move.

He would come out of the gate and be running 15 to 16 lengths off the lead, but all the while, he was clocking the other horses. At the quarter pole he would have gained a little ground and might be eight or nine lengths back; by the eighth pole he would have closed a bit more and would be four or five lengths out of it. But from that point on, unless the leaders were really staying strong, he would just explode and frequently win.

He made a couple hundred thousand dollars for his owners and even won a few stakes races. He was an old pro who had to do it exactly his way. If he were allowed to do that and the race shaped up with the leaders weakening in the stretch, he would win. It was that simple. He knew more about running than I did and he could clock a field better than most jockeys.

Once he developed his own individual pattern, Joel always ran his race no matter what the jockey did or didn't do. Sometimes a jockey might put the whip to him in an effort to get him to make his move a little earlier. It didn't matter. He never changed his game plan. When he felt it was time to give it the big kick he did. If he didn't think it was time, he simply held the pace.

And, just like Hold Old Blue, when the race was over,

he would walk calmly back to the barn, stand quietly for his bath, be rubbed down and cooled out and, at feeding time, lick his feed tub clean.

This old pro had a very successful career and when he started showing some problems with a knee, we retired him. The owners took him home and he became their pet riding horse.

Neither Hold Old Blue nor Joel ever hurt themselves in a race and they never wasted energy. They were true war horses, the kind you could run 15 to 16 times a year and they would stay sound because they knew how to take care of themselves in a race.

Again, it's a matter of knowing your horse. If you have been training a horse since it was two and now it's four or five, you have no excuse for not knowing it well. You should know all of its wants, needs and quirks and, most importantly, you should have adjusted to them.

Once a veteran racehorse has developed its own successful style or pattern of training and running, the worst thing one can do is try to change it. My advice for handling horses like this is to adjust to their needs and then get out of their way.

Above all, assess the horse's ability accurately and accept it for what it is. If the horse runs well at the $30,000 level, leave it there. Don't be trying to push it up in class just because it had a couple of good races and you're wanting a bigger payday. All you will accomplish, usually, is getting the horse beat and hastening the end of its career.

I like to think our stable has been successful over the years, not so much because we have always had a group of great horses, but rather because we've been able to take a large number of average horses and turn them into useful racehorses that have had long and successful careers.

The fact remains, of course, that any horse has only so

many races in it and then it's time for retirement. If we have trained the horse properly and adjusted to its needs, the end of its racing career will not be the end of its usefulness.

As I already mentioned, Joel made a few hundred thousand dollars and then went on to become a family's riding horse. Many ex-racehorses excel in dressage, eventing, jumping, fox hunting, trail riding and even ranch work.

If they've had the necessary traits to become a successful racehorse, those traits will also assure that they will have a successful post-race career.

This is another reason I'm such a strong advocate of gelding all but the great young studs. There are endless opportunities for a retired race gelding, but the options for a stallion unsuited for the breeding barn are limited.

Unbridled, of course, was an exception to my gelding rule. Here was a horse with talent, success and pedigree. He deserved a long and successful career in the stud barn.

Let me turn to Unbridled again as an example of what can happen when campaigning a successful horse at age four and beyond.

We had decided that he had come out of the three-year-old "wars" in great shape, but weren't certain where we should start him for the first race of his four-year-old career. It was early in 1991 and we were in Florida. Craig Perret came out to work Unbridled one morning after we had resumed serious training.

It was just like the year before. The horse was ready and eager to run, those ears twitching as he clocked Craig, waiting, just waiting the signal to cut loose with a burst of speed.

A race that was coming up was the Deputy Minister at Gulfstream Park. It was a seven-furlong sprint and it seemed likely that Housebuster was going to run in it. I didn't want to run him against Housebuster. If Housebuster wasn't entered, I decided, I would let Unbridled have a sprint to start his four-year-old campaign.

However, as it turned out, Housebuster was entered in the race and I changed my mind. I thought about it for a while and decided that if the race truly was what Unbridled needed, he should run, Housebuster or not.

Craig Perret had the call on Housebuster so I asked Pat Day to ride Unbridled.

The race was unbelievable.

At the three-eighths pole, Unbridled was 14 lengths out of it. At the quarter pole he's still nine or 10 lengths back, but he's starting to move. At the eighth pole he's closed to within three lengths and then he just exploded with the most awesome kick I've ever seen and literally shot past Housebuster, one of racing's top sprinters, to win it.

The fans went crazy. As Pat brought him back toward the winner's circle you could mark his progress by the waves of applause that accompanied him, section by section, in the grandstand. These racing fans knew they had witnessed a great athletic feat, a fantastic race with an unbelievable finish, and were paying tribute.

Unbridled came out of the race in fine order and we shipped to Oak Lawn. Then, I made another mistake. I ran him in the mud. Unbridled wanted no part of it and he finished fifth.

It was my mistake, not his.

From there we went to the Pimlico Special in Maryland. Farma Way ran one of his greatest races that day to win it.

For Unbridled, it was a sad day. He bled. Severely. Several days later we had him checked by ultrasound and discovered that he had torn a major lesion in one lung. The examining veterinarian said the horse needed 45 days to recuperate and heal.

The vet also recommended that we gallop Unbridled

during the recuperation period. Galloping, he said, would speed the healing. We just couldn't stress him with fast works.

Here is another example of the class horse that he was. Many racehorses would not have handled just galloping quietly along day after day. They'd have been champing at the bit, wanting to run after a day or two. Not Unbridled. He did just what we asked him to do.

After 45 days, the ultrasound showed the lesion had healed and we were ready to step up the training pace.

Another problem.

He suffered a bruised foot so we lost an additional week as we soaked the bruised foot in a tub and hand walked him. By now, we're into July. Unbridled hasn't raced since the Pimlico Special in May.

I wanted to take him to Del Mar in California for the Pacific Classic, but the lung and foot problems had, I thought, taken that out of consideration. About this time an allowance race opened at Arlington Park for which he qualified. I entered him.

He won it going away, looking like nothing had ever happened to him. He was the Unbridled of old that sent your blood racing when he made his big move down the lane.

I checked him in the barn the next morning. He was relaxed, fit and ready for more action. I looked again at the Pacific Classic. It was only eight days away. Normally, I wouldn't have considered two races that close together, but the allowance race really hadn't been more than a good tightening work for him.

Again, it's a matter of knowing your horse and adjusting to him, his needs and his ability. This horse was ready to run.

I decided to fly him to California for the Pacific Classic.

Unbridled ran a good race in the Classic, finishing a close third with Best Pal winning it. Unbridled came out of the race in fine shape and we returned to Arlington where we freshened him and then moved to Keeneland.

At Keeneland, we freshened him again and then ran him in the Fayette Handicap, where he finished third, as the final prep for that fall's Breeders' Cup Classic at Churchill Downs.

He ran third in the Breeders' Cup Classic. The winner, Black Tie Affair, lead all along and Twilight Agenda, with his tactical speed, finished second. Unbridled had run a good race. Closing gamely on a slow pace, he just wasn't able to collar the front runners.

The time had come to close out his career.

Time to go home.

Unbridled was retired after the 1991 Breeders' Cup Classic and was moved to Gainesway Farm to stand at stud. He had run in 24 races, finishing first, second or third 20 times and had earned in excess of $4 million.

He had nothing more to prove on the racetrack.

As I mentioned earlier, a stable will have horses with long and fruitful careers as long as its goal is to develop horses. By that, I mean the patience to allow a colt or filly to advance at its own pace and not try to make it fit into some predetermined niche.

Once the horse has been developed and is competing, it's time to honestly evaluate the talent with which you are working. If it's a stakes horse, wonderful. If it's an allowance horse, find the right competition. If it doesn't fit either of those categories, it's time to talk about claiming races.

Chapter 15

The Claiming Game

Claiming is a turning game. One moment you own a horse you send to the starting gate, the next minute you don't. Or, the reverse might be true. You might walk onto a racetrack not owning a horse and leave with one in your possession.

It's also a great leveler in Thoroughbred racing as it not only provides slots of competition for horses of varying abilities, but also helps to make certain that the competition remains even.

In its simplest form, claiming means when a group of horses is entered in a $25,000 claiming race, each and every member of that group is for sale at that point in time for $25,000. A properly licensed owner or trainer, who has the purchase price ready to deposit into a special account, has until 15 minutes before post time to enter a claim. If he or she enters a claim, that horse becomes their property when the horses leave the starting gate. There are, of course, specific steps and procedures that must be followed in claiming and we'll get to them shortly.

Allowance races are the next strata up. Generally speaking, the term allowance involves both the weight the horse might carry and the conditions under which it will compete. To achieve parity that will make for a competitive field and challenging betting in a race, the racing secretary will first set forth a list of conditions for a particular race. It might, for example, be for three-year-olds and up who have not yet won a certain amount of money or have not yet won at a particular level of competition. The conditions listed can be about as varied as the racing jurisdictions offering them.

Two key words in allowance races are "other than." The conditions might say that a certain race is for non-winners of a race, other of than maiden, claiming or starting races.

Once you have a group of horses categorized for a particular race, there is another consideration - the amount of weight the horse will carry. An older, more experienced horse with a history of success, might carry 126 pounds for example, while another which is lacking in the above categories might be carrying only 112. The whole purpose is to level the field to make for interesting and competitive racing and wagering.

Horses entered in allowance races can't be claimed. Only in designated claiming races is there a specific provision for horses to change hands.

Claiming races provide a solid foundation for the racing game.

As we mentioned early on, if you want to get into racing quickly and with a lesser investment than that involved in buying and developing our $40,000 yearling, claiming might be the way to go. You can get in quickly and you can get out just as quickly.

However, claiming races also serve another purpose. They provide a level of competition for the horses that aren't good enough to run in allowance or stakes company.

Once I was asked what medication I used to get horses to perform better. The questioner was surprised when I replied, "The best medication I know of to get a better performance out of a horse is a 25,000 cc drop in claiming price. You'll make the owner happy because he'll win a race. You'll make the horse happy because it will run where it wants to run and you'll feel like your training means something for that horse."

In my opinion, medication often defeats itself, but we will get into that a little later.

We have been chronicling various things that might happen with our $40,000 yearling purchase. Let's carry it to the final step. Assume the yearling became a two-year-old that showed promise, but that as a three-year-old, though still trying hard, doesn't have the ability to be an allowance race horse.

You have made a substantial investment in the horse, but it's time to cut yourself loose so you don't spend even more with little or no return on your investment. It's time to look for an appropriate claiming race.

We have already discussed how horses will seek their own level of competition; how a horse that might tear up the competition in a $20,000 claiming race will get "buried" in $50,000 allowance company.

There are subtleties involved in the psychological responses horses have to each other and competition that helps decide at what level and against whom they can be competitive. A case in point is a nice filly we had. We ran her in a race where she finished second to another good filly. They raced each other again, a bit later and our filly got beat again.

One day shortly thereafter at Keeneland we were coming back to the barn with our filly and met the other one leaving for the track. Our filly looked at her and started snorting and blowing and getting all worked up. She knew who that filly was and she knew that filly had dominated her. What I knew was that there would be no point in running them against each other again. Our filly had let me know she'd lose every time. She was intimidated.

What we must do with the $40,000 purchase that didn't make it is find the right level of competition. If we are successful, we might have an opportunity to win a purse or two before someone else steps in and makes a claim.

When you enter a claiming race, you must be prepared to lose your horse to another person without prior notice. Some trainers will try to sneak a good allowance horse into a claiming race as part of a conditioning plan, looking for an easy race and hopeful that no one will notice. That's risky business. I never enter a horse in a claiming race that I don't want claimed.

Generally, I am pretty open with potential purchasers of the horses I run in claiming competition. If someone comes by the barn and wants to see the horse's vet records, I normally will show them after the horse has been claimed.

However, I do have my own little approach to keep them guessing. I run all my claimers in running bandages on the front legs, whether they need them or not. It's just my way of saying nobody gets a free peek at the legs on race day.

The first claiming race in which we enter our prospect that didn't make it will be pretty much guesswork as to entry level. You already know you don't have a horse good enough for allowance company, but you also don't know at what level in the claiming ranks it will do best.

If you enter it in a $25,000 claiming race and it wins flying down the lane 10 lengths in front, you might try upping it to the $40,000 level next time. If, on the other hand, the horse gets beat by 10 lengths, you better be thinking about dropping to a lower level.

You keep trying until you find a slot where the horse is competitive, campaign it there and wait for a new owner to come along.

Can money be made claiming horses?

The answer is yes, but you have to pretty much concentrate on that aspect of racing. Our stable is more concerned with the development of allowance and stakes horses. When we put a horse in a claiming race, normally, it's because it doesn't fit our program and we want to move it along to make room for another prospect.

This type of horse may be sound and have ability at a certain level; it just no longer fits our program.

Someone might come along at Arlington Park and claim this horse from us, move to Hawthorne where the competition isn't as keen and provide the horse with an opportunity for success at that level.

In that scenario everybody wins. Our stable loses a horse, but brings in a new prospect; another trainer has a horse that fits his or her program at Hawthorne in easier company, and the horse has a chance to be a racing success at a level where it's comfortable.

As I mentioned earlier, there are some specific rules involved in claiming a horse and if you plan to go that route, you must background yourself thoroughly.

First of all, normally the man on the street can't walk in and claim a horse. Though it's possible in some places, at most jurisdictions you must be a licensed owner or trainer to claim a horse. Secondly, you must post the money up front. In most jurisdictions, a personal check won't do. You must have the cash or a certified check to place in a holding account.

You must file your claim with the official in charge at least 15 minutes before the race. Each track has office space set aside and an official in charge to handle claims. Once you file a claim and it's duly recorded, the wheels of ownership are set into motion and you are locked into that horse, win or lose once it leaves the starting gate.

If the horse gets on the board, the previous owner gets that day's purse money. Once it leaves the starting gate, you get the horse, no matter how it finishes the race. If it breaks a leg at the quarter-pole and has to be destroyed, it's still your horse. If it suffers an injury that requires a year of recuperation, it's your horse and your expense.

At some jurisdictions you can buy claiming insurance as a protective measure, but regardless of what you do, the horse is yours once it leaves the starting gate if you've filed a legitimate claim. If, however, something happens in the post parade or prior to the start and the horse is scratched, your claim is invalidated.

You take possession of the horse as soon as the race is over. If the horse is required to go to the test barn, the previous owner must see it through that procedure and then turn the horse over to the new owner. If it doesn't go to the test barn, the horse will change hands in the paddock after it's unsaddled.

As the buyer, you are responsible for informing yourself about the horse independently. If, for example, you claim a horse that is listed in the program as a stallion, but turns out to be a gelding, that is your problem. The fact that someone else made a mistake doesn't let you off the hook. You are expected to verify everything you want to know about the horse independently.

In an effort to prevent horses from being popped from track to track via the claiming route, most jurisdictions have specific rules about when, where and at what level you run the horse you've claimed. Normally, for example, you can't run it in a cheaper claiming race until at least 30 days have elapsed between purchase and the cheaper race.

During those 30 days you will have to run the horse at 25 percent more than it was claimed for. In other words, if you claimed a horse for $10,000, you might have to run it back at $12,500 if you wanted to race within 30 days of making the claim.

You may also be required to keep the horse at the track where it was claimed until that meet ends. That rule is designed to prevent people from picking off claiming horses at a major track one day and shipping them to a lesser track for some quick wins a few days later.

You also must keep the horse in the ownership name in which it was claimed for 30 days.

Remember, the rules vary from jurisdiction to jurisdiction. Know what they are when you file your claim.

Still another rule involves equipment. You are obligated to run the horse in exactly the same equipment as was being used when it was claimed unless you get permission to make a change from the stewards. If, for example, you claim a horse that was running in blinkers and you think they are a deterrent rather than a help, you have to follow procedure to get them removed.

First you will notify the starting crew that you are seeking the change. Then, during a morning training session, you will start the horse from the gate without blinkers. If the starter feels the horse handled the test adequately, he will sign a card to that effect. That card must be presented to the track stewards for approval. When they give their okay, the blinkers can come off. The next time you enter the horse, you must note on the entry form that it is running with the blinkers off.

The same procedure is followed in the event you want to add equipment that the horse was not carrying when claimed. It must be approved by the starter and the stewards through the same steps involved in removing equipment.

Claiming is a special kind of risk because it's no secret that some owners and trainers use this route to get rid of horses that might be in the process of becoming unsound or have reached the end of their racing usefulness. While some trainers will level with you about this horse or that in a claiming race, they have no obligation to do so and you can't bring in a veterinarian for your own pre-race examination.

It's a case of buyer beware.

Yet, I still believe that it remains a good opportunity to get involved in racing at the specific level of investment you

195

desire.

If you do decide to try the claiming game, don't have unreasonable expectations. Most trainers aren't dumb. Normally, they are running their claiming horses at their level of ability. Don't expect to pick up a $20,000 claimer and be competing in $50,000 allowance races a few weeks down the road. It can happen, but don't count on it.

Most of the horses claimed from our stable end up running for their new owners at about the same level at which they were claimed.

One exception I can think of was a nice little filly that just didn't fit into our program so we put her in a claiming race and she was picked up by a trainer with a small stable. He spent a lot of time with her and wound up trying her on the turf, which she liked. She had some temporary success for him as she qualified for conditions in races that were just right for her. After moving through that set of conditions, however, she settled back to the claiming level where he had obtained ownership. In the meantime, however, he had been successful picking up some wins that translated into purse money.

There are a number of success stories out there, but very seldom will you claim a horse and make a dramatic turnaround with it.

Of course, the point remains that everything about horse racing is a risk. Our $40,000 yearling might appreciate to be worth a million if it is a major stakes winner. On the other hand, if things go wrong, we might wind up running it in a $20,000 claiming race and be happy to do so. You should know that at the outset and be prepared mentally and financially to handle either circumstance.

This is why claiming is so important to racing. As the initial investor, you might wind up having more than $100,000 invested in the $40,000 yearling and a couple years later haven't seen anything in return if that horse was not properly managed. By now you know that you can't possibly recoup by competing in a series of low end races because your entry level investment was too high. At this point you must choose to lose the horse in a claiming race and cut losses.

When you do that and the horse is claimed, however, the new owner has invested only $20,000 and, by comparison, his options, if the horse is sound and has some ability, are expanded. This just might be a solid runner at the $20,000 claiming level and become somebody's "big" horse at a small track.

Sometimes fillies are claimed because someone looks at the pedigree and decides she would nick perfectly with a stallion he or she might have. Still others are claimed off the track for the show ring - hunter-jumper competition, eventing or dressage.

If I were claiming, I would want to claim horses off the most successful trainer I could find. Generally speaking, this trainer is going to be dealing with a high class set of horses and he might be sending one to the claiming ranks because it just isn't meshing with the program he's carrying out. You know that the horse from the successful stable will have been fed well and trained properly.

Our stable has been known to move a fair number of horses through the claiming ranks at the end of a summer at Arlington Park because we are preparing to spend the winter at Gulfstream Park in Florida where conditions are tighter and competition tougher. It is pointless for us to take horses of lesser ability to Florida and enter them in competition they can't handle. It costs the owner money that won't be recouped and can destroy the horse's competitive desire. At a time like this, it's an excellent opportunity for someone to pick up good horses from our stable that will win in lesser competition.

There are those that would say to me, if these horses can be winners at a lower level, why don't you just create another string of your own for them? The answer is that a trainer can only spread himself so thin. Our goal is to develop winning allowance and stakes horses and that's where we focus our attention and effort.

Let me repeat the bottom line warning: most claimers are at the claiming level for a reason. They are starting to have soundness problems, they are getting near the end of their career because of age, they don't have ability, or they are lacking in class.

Before arriving at the claiming level with our $40,000 purchase, however, we will have taken the time and had the patience to develop this horse at its own pace to make certain that we didn't short-change it in any way.

Patience.

Patience.

Patience.

You must be patient if you're going to develop horses.

There is another necessary ingredient that often gets overlooked as we work patiently to develop our young prospects.

Barn help.

You as a trainer and an owner can only be as good as the people with which you surround yourself.

Chapter 16

Good Help a Key Ingredient to Success

Hiring and keeping good employees on the shedrow is an important ingredient in any trainer's success story. To be a success, you must surround yourself with people who want to be where they are. To accomplish that you must create a pleasant and positive working environment.

A clean, neat shedrow will naturally eliminate certain people that you don't want to deal with anyway. If everyone else is neat and clean, the slob will be out of place and want to be elsewhere, which is just where you want him or her to be.

A key bit of advice, don't overwork your help. Think of them in the same context as you think of yourself. You can do so much and then you begin to burn out. The same is true of your help, only more so because they might not be as motivated as you are.

You must be a judge of character and ability when hiring and assigning certain employees to specific tasks. Not everyone is suited to do the same thing. You might take the best groom in the world and promote him to barn foreman and be shocked to discover he can't begin to handle the responsibility.

Know your help.

My wife, Wanda, and I have as our desire and goal, the development of both horses and people to their fullest potential.

Just like racehorses, shedrow workers have to learn to cope with stress and pressure. To keep stress and pressure at a minimum, you have to have a proper chain of command.

In our stable, the chain of command starts with the trainer. Next comes the assistant trainer, then the barn foreman, the grooms, the exercise riders and the hot walkers. Also included is the administrative assistant who is responsible for maintaining all of our computerized records and the night watchman who must also be a person who knows and understands horses.

The assistant trainer is just that. He or she is in charge of the day to day operation of the stable. They report to me. Any assistant trainer, except for one, that I have ever had has worked his or her way up through the ranks at least from the barn foreman level. Only after he or she has experienced what the other jobs are like by overseeing them from the barn foreman's position, can they truly comprehend the complete shedrow picture.

Reporting to the assistant trainer is the barn foreman. He is in charge of all of the other employees except the exercise riders who report to the assistant trainer.

Let's take a look at the employees on a shedrow, along with their responsibilities. One of the most important people on any shedrow is the groom. This is the person who is responsible for keeping a horse clean and happy. Each of our grooms is responsible for three horses. We make an effort to match grooms with horses with which they can establish rapport.

The entry position at our stable is the hot walker-bucket washer. This is a person who is an assistant to the groom. The hot walker doesn't do all that much walking of horses, but he or she will hold them while the groom is bathing the horse, will scrub out water pails and feed tubs, clean and rake the walking paths around the shedrow and just, generally, do anything required in helping the groom keep the horses healthy and happy.

The assistant groom assists while the groom gives the horse its bath after a morning workout.
Photo by Les Sellnow

Daily routine.

Grooms will arrive at the barn at 4:30 to 5:00 a.m. Their first job will be to clean the stalls of manure and urine-soaked straw. I believe in a quiet, peaceful shedrow, so radios are not allowed in the mornings. I want both people and horses to be concentrating on the business at hand and not be distracted. Blaring radios are a distraction. Also, I do not want someone walking a horse or working on the shedrow with cassette earphones in their ears.

There are three ways to cause an accident: not to see a potential problem; not to hear it and not to care. A person can't always see what's happening behind them or out of their line of vision. When that's the case you have to depend on your ears. If your ears are plugged into a cassette player, you aren't going to hear anything until it's too late, so no earphones on our shedrow.

I want every stall in the barn cleaned before the first horse goes to the track. Then, when the horse is out with its set, the groom can shake up the bedding and put down fresh straw to replace that which was removed earlier.

When a horse returns from the track, I want it to walk into a clean, freshly bedded stall after being bathed, rubbed down and cooled out. By this time, the hot walker has also scrubbed buckets and has fresh drinking water waiting. As a treat, each horse will also have a small amount of alfalfa to munch on in the corner of the stall.

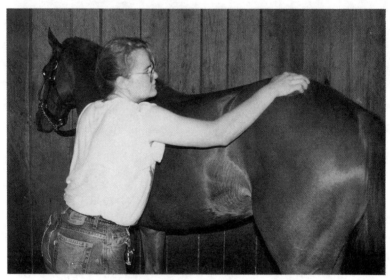

The only way to make a horse's coat shine is with a vigorous daily grooming.   *Photo by Les Sellnow*

It is also the groom's job to thoroughly brush and curry that horse's coat before it goes to the track. We want that coat to glisten and shine and the only way to achieve that is with vigorous grooming that removes dust, dirt and dead hair and brings the skin's natural oils to the surface.

The groom will also saddle and bridle the horse for the exercise rider. When the horse returns from the track, the hot walker holds it while the groom gives it a bath, rubs it down and then walks it out until it is ready to be returned to the stall where a full hay net of grass hay is waiting.

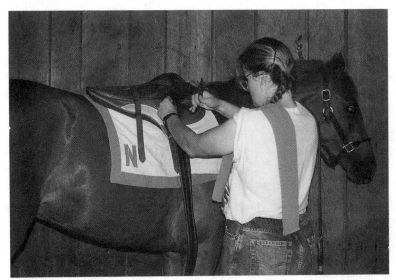

It is the groom's job to saddle the horse for the exercise rider. *Photo by Les Sellnow*

No one spends more time with a horse than the groom and, as a result, the groom knows every little quirk of the animal's personality. This means the groom is a valuable resource for the trainer in determining the horse's likes and needs. We expect the grooms to communicate any change in the horse's personality or any change in its reaction to daily routine. Does it clean up its food every day? Is a colt getting nippy and anxious? Does the horse relax and let down during a bath and rubdown following a training session? Is there any change in excretions of manure and urine? Does it stand with its head outside the stall door, curious and interested in what's going on or does it sulk in a corner?

Those may seem like relatively minor details, but by paying attention to them everyone stays attuned to the horse's wants and needs. And that, as we've been saying all along, is essential if you're to have a successful racehorse.

One thing we do that is different from many stables is feed grain and supplements after all the horses have been worked each morning. The customary thing to do is to feed very early, about 3:30 a.m., before taking the horses out for training sessions.

In my opinion, this is the wrong approach. Just like people, some horses are slow eaters and some are fast eaters. I have some horses that clean up their feed tub in a matter of minutes and others that dawdle over it for an hour or more. If you feed before taking them out for training, you are trapping yourself into a schedule where all horses have to be finished eating at the same time. If you wait until after training, each horse can consume its food at its leisure.

We do not have a feed crew as such. Preparing the ration for each horse is an incentive job. Whomever wants to make some extra money can volunteer for it. Each horse has its individual ration and it is prepared in that horse's feed tub before feeding time.

Doing the laundry is also an incentive job - washing bandages and blankets. We have no one assigned to the task, but persons volunteering for it receive extra pay.

Still another incentive job is being a pony rider. Pony riders are the people who, on race day, lead the horse onto the track after it's saddled and to the starting gate when it's post time. Independent pony riders who furnish their own horses are available and are paid a flat rate per horse led. However, we often like to have our horses handled by our own people riding a pony with which the horse is already familiar.

Under our incentive program, we furnish the horse and pay the person on our staff, usually one of the exercise riders, 50 percent of the going rate as all they have to provide are themselves, their skill and their time.

Another incentive job is caring for the pony on a daily basis. No groom is assigned to the pony, but the person who volunteers for that incentive job cares for the pony just like a groom would a racehorse. The stall is cleaned and rebedded, the horse is bathed, rubbed down and cooled out.

On race day afternoons, however, if the pony is used by an exercise rider for getting horses to the starting gate, then he or she is responsible for that pony's total care at the end of the day.

Providing incentive jobs helps you get a good reading on which employees have a desire to advance beyond their current positions and which ones don't really care.

As I mentioned earlier, the grooms and hot walkers report to the barn foreman. He has the additional responsibility for any leg wraps, poultices or rubs that are put on the horses as well as being in charge of any other type of physical therapy, such as ice tubs, foot tubs and the like. He is constantly checking legs and communicating with the grooms about any change they might have been observed in the horse's behavior.

I do not depend on the grooms to report unsoundness, although they often do, which is appreciated. That is not their job and most of them are not trained to detect and understand various types of lameness. Their job is to keep that horse clean and happy.

The barn foreman and the assistant trainer should know legs as well as I do. Soundness is our responsibility.

The grooms have to show up early, about 4:30 a.m., at our stable, but they also get off early. To ease their work load, we have established the buddy system. Each groom has a partner - a "buddy" - with whom they rotate afternoon feeding chores. If they do not have to feed in the afternoon or their "buddy" does not have a horse in a race that afternoon, their work day will be over by about 11:00 a.m.

If a groom or his "buddy" has a horse in a race, both will report to work that afternoon to assist in both pre-race and post-race care. While the groom leads the horse to the saddling paddock, the buddy shakes down and freshens the horse's stall, draws hot water for a bath and has everything ready for the horse's return to the barn after the race. Once the race has been run and the horse returned to the barn, the buddy is free to go as the groom and hot walker handle the bathing, rubbing down and cooling out.

We operate on a six-day work week, but also attempt to allow everyone to have off every other afternoon. We have a "swing" groom who fills in during days off. We also insist that everyone take a vacation. Our employees get one week of paid vacation the first year and two weeks after two years and thereafter.

It's the barn foreman's job to evaluate the work of the grooms and hot walkers and take action if they are not fulfilling their responsibilities. If a groom doesn't show up for work, it's the barn foreman's job to find out why. It is also his responsibility to establish and regulate working hours for the grooms and hot walkers.

Because of their responsibilities, the barn foremen often find it difficult to get days off or take vacations during a race meet. When that happens, they might accumulate vacation time and when things slow down in the winter, take a month or more off.

The barn foreman reports directly to the assistant trainer who is my eyes, ears and voice. As I mentioned, assistant trainers at our stable work their way up through the ranks so they know and understand every facet of our system.

The assistant trainer reports to me. It's his job to know and understand each horse in the stable as well as I do. He is my first line of information concerning a horse's mental attitude, soundness, immune system and ability. It is his responsibility to advise me of any changes.

If something is amiss among the shedrow staff, it's the assistant trainer's job to be aware of it. He then takes up the matter with the barn foreman who will carry out whatever directive is issued to solve the problem.

It is important that the chain of command remain intact. I talk to the grooms, the hot walkers and everyone else on shedrow, but if I spot something I don't like that is being done by a groom, for example, I don't attempt to correct that person on the spot. Instead, I'll discuss the matter with the barn foreman and let him handle it.

I never insert myself or my authority between the assistant trainer or barn foreman and the help.

The assistant trainer has to be capable of doing everything I do. In our operation, this is extremely important because at times, especially in the summer, we may be operating out of three locations at once. We may have a string of horses in Louisville; another group in Chicago and a third set in Saratoga. Each location will have a complete shedrow staff. Obviously, I can't be three places at once so I need assistant trainers I can trust.

I need a person who can make responsible decisions on the spot, talk to owners when they call, hire exercise riders, monitor a horse's progress and communicate it to me in such a way that I can keep tabs on that animal almost as though I were there. That is why it is so important that the assistant trainer work his way up through the ranks.

Only once did I vary from this rule of never hiring an assistant trainer who hadn't first been at least a barn foreman. It didn't work. The man I hired didn't know how to handle people. Being a barn foreman is not an easy job. A good barn foreman knows how to deal with people and keep employees both productive and happy. If he is a success in that capacity and knows and understands horses, it's highly likely that he would be a good candidate for assistant trainer. If he cannot handle people well at that level, he will never make a good assistant trainer, no matter how well he knows and understands horses.

While the assistant trainer does everything I do, he doesn't have the burden of worrying about the financial management of the business - keeping the IRS happy, paying workman's compensation insurance, social security and a myriad of other financial details.

He also does not have to worry about the major decisions on where we're going to run and when. That remains my responsibility.

It is the assistant trainer's job to hire exercise riders and to instruct them in what should be done with each horse on a given day. Most tracks open for training at 5:30 a.m. or earlier. By opening time we want our exercise riders on hand, limbered up and ready to ride. We want all of our stalls cleaned and the first set of horses ready to head for the track.

The exercise rider is the most specialized person on the staff. His or her one and only job is to ride the horses. They are also charged with the responsibility of keeping tack clean, oiled and in good order. When they have finished riding for the morning and have cleaned their tack, they are free to leave.

Figuring out how to give riders days off is a little more difficult than grooms and hot walkers because of the demands of training schedules. Some riders like to accumulate free time so they can have a more lengthy breather and we seek to accommodate them as the schedule permits.

Generally speaking, there is a difference in the way grooms, hot walkers and exercise riders handle days off. In our shedrow, it is not at all uncommon for a groom or hot walker to be hanging around on the shedrow on a day off, drinking coffee and just visiting with the people who are working. The shedrow is where they are comfortable, thus, they spend much of their free time there. They seem to enjoy the fact that they can sleep in and not have any specific responsibilities one day a week but, at the same time, they are content to spend that day with their friends on the shedrow.

Exercise riders are more apt to be off doing their own thing on free days.

Overall, our goal is to make the shedrow an efficient, attractive and harmonious work place. We try to add extra little touches like planting flowers around the barn and, of course, keeping the entire area neat and clean. I don't want an owner arriving at our shedrow being forced to step around manure buckets or debris. Nor do I want them to have to listen to radios blaring or the help arguing.

I also believe in a shedrow that has no secrets from the owner.

One of the questions always raised by the help is this: "What should I tell the owner if he asks about his horse."

My answer is, "Tell him or her the truth. You can't get into trouble if you tell the truth."

If you, as an owner, find out that someone on the shedrow is feeding you misinformation about your horse, be it a foreman, assistant trainer or the trainer, it is time to move your horse.

Not permitted on our shedrow are drinking or drugs. Occasionally we'll host a picnic and will buy a case of beer, but we are also well aware that there are people on the backside who are fighting to conquer alcohol problems. We make certain that any gathering has an abundance of soft drinks.

Our attitude on alcohol is that we don't mind a person having a mixed drink or a cold beer, we just insist that they don't do so on the shedrow whether working or visiting. It's a simple, but hard and fast rule. No alcohol in the shedrow.

Another rule that we enforce is punctuality. We like to let people work at their own pace as long as they can have their horses ready when it's training time, but we do insist that they get to work on time. Once they are on the job, we let them proceed at a pace that is comfortable for them. Some grooms might be done at 10:30 and others might still be there working at 11:30. As long as they are getting the job done and aren't hindering the normal flow of activity and scheduling, they can work at their own pace.

We want our shedrow to be clean, attractive, quiet and safe. If you, as the owner of our hypothetical $40,000 yearling, visit our shedrow at any time of the day or evening, we want you to be impressed with the fact that your horse is getting the best of care in a clean, safe environment with dedicated people in charge.

If a trainer enforces the basic rules regarding cleanliness, alcohol, noise, drugs and punctuality, he or she will be setting a standard that only quality people will try to meet. In other words, the drunk and the guy or girl smoking pot, won't want to work there because they would stick out like a sore thumb. They know they would be out of a job almost before they began, so they steer clear of the well-run shedrow. What you wind up with then, are people who appreciate a clean, safe environment and who have a genuine love and concern for the horses.

Racing, being the game that it is and racehorses being animals that need care 365 days of the year, we can't treat holidays like most other businesses or professions. Horses need to be fed whether it's Christmas, New Year's or Easter.

However, we do keep the workload at a bare minimum over Christmas and New Year's. Horses don't go to the track on those days. The most we will do is walk them in the shedrow.

Before leaving the shedrow help, we must discuss another key person in our operation - the administrative assistant. The modern world of computers enables today's trainer to run a more efficient operation than in the past. It is the job of the administrative assistant to not only keep tabs on such things as payroll, workman's compensation and such, but to record on the computer everything that occurs with a horse in our stable.

I want to be able to go to the computer, call up a horse by name and have presented before me everything from that horse's training and race record to when it was shod and its complete health record. Everything that can help us keep a better handle on that horse and its progress in the training program is recorded and available for immediate retrieval.

The final person on our staff is the night watchman. His job is just what the name implies. He keeps watch over the barn from the time everyone else leaves in the evening until the first groom arrives in the morning.

His hands on work with the horses will be to pull feed tubs from the stalls in the evening after feeding. As a tub is cleaned up by the horse, he will remove it. If a horse isn't cleaning up its feed, the night watchman will leave the tub in the stall until about an hour before the groom shows up. He will also leave a note behind, calling attention to which horse did not clean up its feed and how much was left.

It is also the job of the night watchman, if need be, to muzzle a horse that has a tendency to gorge itself on hay or straw all night long. A horse like that is muzzled about midnight or 1:00 a.m. so that it doesn't head to the track for a morning training session with a full stomach.

In summary, we try to operate the shedrow on the premise that responsibilities are outlined for each position. The person holding that position is expected to carry them out without having someone constantly looking over his or her shoulder.

I remember someone being surprised that I didn't go back to the shedrow to get a horse for a particular race. My reply was, "If I have to go back to the shedrow to make sure everything's being done right at this point, it's time to fire somebody."

We find that by having an attractive, clean and efficient shedrow populated by dedicated workers, there is little need for firing or reprimands.

I want the people around me to be happy and to have something to look forward to as far as improving themselves is concerned. Wage increases are also used as incentives. We have a starting pay rate with a raise after two months and another increase after six months with annual raises after that, providing everything is working out well. There is also the opportunity to share in the earnings of the stable.

Our goal is to pay our help enough so they aren't forced to live in track dormitories. They can afford to live off the grounds if they so desire.

There are few things more important than good help on the back side.

Another integral member of a racing crew, but normally not one on the regular payroll is the jockey. There are times when a jockey can make the difference between winning and losing. Let's take a look at what's involved in keeping trainer and jockey on the same wave lengths.

Chapter 17

Working with Jockeys

Use good jockeys, don't let jockeys use you.

Sound a bit too simplistic? Not if you think about it. A jockey has one way to make money. Winning races. The good ones know how to do this. That's why they are in demand.

A trainer's job is to train and develop horses. Sometimes this goal conflicts with the jockey's. The trainer knows that one race doesn't make or break a horse. How a horse comes out of a race is more important in the long run than where it finished. For the jockey, on the other hand, where his or her horse finishes in a given race determines how much money is earned.

When you select a jockey, you want to be confident that he or she is going to ride your horse the way you want it ridden, not just attempt to notch another winning statistic. If the horse is a front runner, you want to feel confident that you have a jockey that will hustle it out of the gate and onto the lead. If it's a horse that comes from off the pace, you want to rest assured that the move will be made at the right time.

It's the trainer' job to not only know the jockeys and their ability levels, but also to know what you can expect of them in the way of commitment as a campaign unfolds. We might, for example, be able to get a particular well-known jockey to ride our $40,000 prospect in an allowance race that is a prep for a major stake, only to find when the stake race rolls around that the jockey has committed to ride a different horse that may have a better chance of winning.

We might have been better served in this case to have contracted with a lesser known jockey who would agree to stay with the prospect through both races, if our horse is not an exceptional runner, getting to know its quirks and style of running.

The agreement between jockey and trainer is a private contract, usually negotiated by the jockey's agent on a race by race basis. The jockeys whose horses finish first, second or third get a percentage of the winnings. Jockeys whose horses don't get on the board, are paid a predetermined amount to make the ride.

While it is the trainer's responsibility to have a horse fit and ready to run its best, there is little doubt that a jockey can be a determining factor as to whether that happens. The trainer has to know his horse and know the jockeys in order to consistently try to make the right match.

Some jockeys are super at getting a horse out of the gate, for instance. Others are tops at getting a horse to settle and certain top jockeys have that unbelievable feel for when to wait on a horse and when to make a move. They know in a split second when the time is right and move instinctively.

Again, you can use a boxer as a comparison. If the guy looks at his opponent and thinks, now is the time to throw this particular punch, it's already too late. He has to feel when the time is right and let fly on instinct.

Back to my opening statement about not letting the jockeys use you. What I'm trying to say here is that when a jockey is at or near the top of the standings, he or she wants to stay there. Let's use as an example a timid filly that you have finally gotten trained and ready to run a good strong race. What she needs in an upcoming out is a jockey who will let her relax and run her race.

What you don't want is for the jockey to be making a wrong move at the wrong time. Maybe he decides, what the heck, front running speed is holding up today; might as well move her early and hope she can get in front and hold on to win. What is likely to happen if he moves too early with this filly is she may get the lead, but probably won't hold it and will have her confidence badly shaken when she's passed in the stretch. When the race is over, instead of having a confident filly that ran within her comfort zone, you have a filly that had her cage rattled and is now unsure of herself. The next morning you find that she hasn't touched her feed and is a basket case mentally. You face weeks of painstaking work to get her back to where she was prior to that abortive effort.

I never run a horse that I don't want to win, but I fully admit that I have run a lot of horses where my chief concern has been with how they came out of the race, rather than where they finished.

If the jockey, in our example above, had waited on the filly as we wanted, he still may have gotten the win and you would have a confident, improving filly with which to go on. You want the jockey to do what is right by the horse, not only for the race that particular day, but for races in the future.

Let me further illustrate my point with a story about a horse named Star Choice and jockey Jim McKnight. Star Choice was owned by the Genter stable and was having a very good year. So good, that he had set one track record and we decided to take him to California for the Breeders' Cup.

Some of the top jockeys who didn't have a horse for that race, started calling me and the Genters, saying they would like to ride Star Choice. I said that Jim McKnight had been riding the horse and I wanted to stick with him because he knew the horse and, though he may not have as big a name as some of the jockeys making inquiry, he knew Star Choice best and I wanted him aboard.

215

Don McBeth was the first jockey to really get a handle on Star Choice and he rode him only once. He shared this important information with me and I had passed it on to McKnight. Don was on Star Choice in a stakes race at a mile and one-eighth. We thought the horse could handle the distance and would have a big finishing kick from the quarter-pole on. Following my instructions, Don asked Star Choice for run at the quarter pole and got it. By the time they reached the eighth pole, Star Choice was third. Just as quickly as he'd moved up, he faded, finishing fifth.

"I don't know what happened," I told McBeth after the race. "This horse is fit and ready to run."

"Carl," he said, "this is a talented horse and he can run, but he can only run a mile on the turf and in that mile his kick is going to be for an eighth of a mile not a quarter."

He was right.

Jim McKnight now knew that as well and I knew that I could trust Jim to sit chilly on that horse and not be dissuaded from his game plan no matter what happened in front of him. I wasn't so sure that would be the case with some of the jockeys seeking the mount in the Breeders' Cup race.

In the Breeders' Cup, Star Choice hustled out of the gate in good order and was laying right where we wanted him, about fourth or fifth back. As the race unfolded, he remained there. However, as the field bunched for home, he appeared to be in trouble. He had no running room. Jim didn't move on him. Just sat there, though he was boxed in on the rail.

Finally, a small hole opened when they reached the eighth pole and Star Choice shot through it and came running. He finished second.

The point is this. Most jockeys would have made a move earlier, when they realized they were boxed in. They would have tried to get out of the predicament by going outside or attempting to force the horse through the pack. If that had

216

been done, Star Choice would have responded, but wouldn't have had anything left for the finish.

Jim McKnight had the courage to stay with the game plan and hope for a hole, knowing that the horse had an eighth of a mile to run, and its only true chance of getting on the board was to use this run at the latest possible moment .

Communication.

A trainer and a jockey have to communicate. The truth is that most horses have a certain distance where they can give it their all-out effort. For some it's a quarter of a mile for others, it's an eighth or whatever.

This particular capability is sometimes tricky to figure because it may vary with the company the horse is in. Running in easy allowance company, a quarter mile kick might be spread out for half a mile, while in a stakes race against higher quality horses, it might be reduced to half that.

I remember John Nerud being asked if the great Dr. Fager could run a mile and a quarter. "Sure," he said, "he could run two miles in the right company."

Lest it sound like the trainer has to provide a blueprint for the jockey in each race, let me hasten to say that this is far from the truth. If you have to literally tell a jockey how to ride a race, you have made a poor choice for a jockey.

Tell him or her the quirks of the horse and what you want done, but don't give detailed instructions on how to ride the race. In the case of a horse like Star Choice, about all you would say is, "Remember, this horse can close for an eighth of a mile and no more." Or, you might tell the jockey on another horse in another race, "I'd like to see this filly off the pace in the early going" or, with another individual, "She needs to be pushed a little from the start to keep her on the pace."

217

A jockey and trainer must have good communication. Carl Nafzger and Brian Peck confer in the paddock before a race at Churchill Downs.
Photo by Les Sellnow

If there is something specific to say about your horse, say it in the paddock, but then let the jockey and his or her instincts take over. Keep the instructions basic and simple, because there are too many unknowns and too many uncontrollable factors that can only be handled and analyzed as they arise.

Suppose, for example, your whole race strategy is to get out of the gate first. Every bit of strategy discussed and decided on is predicated on your horse being in the lead at the first call. Only your horse is caught napping when the gate opens and instead of being first, is in the middle of the pack and running fifth after the first quarter. All those best laid plans have gone up in smoke in a matter of seconds and the jockey has to adjust to the situation he or she is in, not what you had planned.

Let the jockey know basically what you want done and fill him or her in on any of the horse's quirks and then step back and let them ride the race. The good jockeys will pay attention to what you suggest and seek to ride accordingly. If they don't respect you enough to listen to basic instructions, then you have the wrong jockey.

Use a jockey that works with you, not one who works for you.

The more a jockey rides your particular horse, the better he or she gets to know it and fewer instructions are needed. I have already mentioned my instructions to Craig Perret with Unbridled on Derby Day. "You know the horse, Craig."

When a race is over, you'll see trainer and jockey huddling for a few minutes. This is an important time and a trainer should be prepared to listen, especially if you're dealing with a class jockey who gets an instant feel for a horse like Don McBeth did in just one race on Star Choice. By listening to him that day, we learned a good deal about Star Choice and put it to good use. You train the horse day by day and get to know it well, but only the jockey can feel what happens in a race.

There will be times, however, when that little meeting isn't so pleasant. A time, for example, when, though being told to come from off the pace, a jockey has hustled your horse to the lead the first jump out of the gate and had a horrible trip. There is no patented way to handle such a situation. Personally, I admit that sometimes I explode at the jockey. Other times, I'm angry, but quiet. If I think the jockey has made an honest mistake, I just quietly tell him or her, "No problem, we'll do better next time."

If the jockey has done exactly as you instructed and the

horse finished out of it, it is time to point the finger the other way. You, as the trainer, made a mistake. It won't do any good to yell at the jockey for finishing in back of the pack. It's time for you to make an adjustment in training and race strategy.

A trainer has to accept the fact that he or she is unable to do anything to help the horse from the time you boost that jockey into the saddle until they cross the finish line. All you can do is watch, wait and hope.

How you watch a race as a trainer, however, can have a bearing on what you learn or don't learn about your horse. I know people who like to watch through wide angle binoculars so they can keep the entire field in sight and compare how their horse is doing in respect to the others. For my part, I could watch a race with a telescope. All I'm really interested in is my horse; what it's doing and what the jockey's doing.

By this time, unless it's a starter race for a youngster, I know my horse and how it runs. I know when it should move and when it shouldn't. I want to be evaluating my horse stride by stride so that if something does go wrong, I'll understand it and know how to correct the problem.

I'll also be watching where the jockey's hands are. I want to know what he has to do to either keep the horse "alive" or to act as a calming influence.

The trainer's job is to sit there during a race and evaluate. The jockey's job is to execute; doing what has to be done to get a win if the race shapes up to make that possible, but doing it in such a way that the horse comes back unharmed and confident, ready to run another day.

A good jockey is like a master card player. The top card player not only knows what's in his hand, but is adept at "reading" what everyone else is holding. Well, a good jockey is not only rating and reading his horse, he's also reading all of the horses in front and even behind him. He is going to sense when a particular horse will weaken or make a move and he will be ready to either take advantage of, or counter that move.

Normally, you will never go into a race that you don't have a chance of winning, but there will be times when you know full well that everything has to shape up just right for you to have a chance. This, again, is important information to pass on to the jockey.

I remember a big, kind of awkward two-year-old that we had entered in a race at Arlington, but he certainly wasn't favored to win. The favorite that day deserved to be just that. He was a horse with brilliant speed. To try to match our colt's speed against his would have been suicide.

I told the jockey, "There's no way we can match that front running colt's speed. Just lay back and see what happens. Don't get caught in the speed, make your move when you think the time's right."

Well, it was a textbook case of everything shaping up right for us. Every other horse in the field took a shot at that fast colt on the lead until they had burned out themselves and him as well. In the meantime, our big ol' colt had been just galloping along behind them. Down the stretch, the whole field, including the speed colt, faltered and our horse put in a late run and won the race.

Not only had our colt got on the board, but he'd learned a lot about running. He'd taken dirt in the face while trailing and had gotten a big confidence boost by finding out he could pass the front runners in the stretch.

It was a win, win situation for us and the jockey as well. We both got some purse money and our horse was a better, more confident runner in the future. If we hadn't accepted the fact that we could not keep up with the speed horses and sent the colt after them, he not only wouldn't won, but would have had his confidence shaken besides.

The thing to remember about jockeys is this. All the

good ones will want the mount on your 8-5 favorite. Don't be swayed by the fact that a name jockey wants your horse in a particular race. Find out if he truly wants to be involved with the horse during a campaign or if this is just a chance to notch another quick statistic along with a paycheck.

There's a lot of debate going on now about whip use. There are those who advocate doing away with the stick altogether. I don't agree with that. I don't want a stick happy jockey that is going to pound on my horses, but I do want the jockey to have the option of using it when needed.

I think stewards might be a little more strict concerning over-use of the stick, but I would not want to see it outlawed. There simply are some horses that need to be woke up at a certain point in a race. It should be used as a motivational tool and as such is not an instrument of abuse. However, if a rider is coming down the lane on a tired horse and the jockey is slashing away with his stick, the stewards should take action. You can't beat speed into a horse after it's given all it has to give.

A stick is an essential tool for the jockey when a horse starts to drift out or in during a race. That's when you'll see the jockey reach up there where the horse can see it and shake that stick in his face to stop the drift. In that circumstance, the stick becomes a safety tool.

Sometimes in a race, a horse's attention wanders from the jockey. He may be barreling down the stretch and decide that the crowd should get his attention instead of the race. At a time like that, a sharp crack from the stick will help that horse focus his attention where it should be; on running not gawking at the crowd.

In another situation, a young horse might be coming down the stretch in the lead and suddenly realize for the first time that there are 20,000 screaming people in the stands along the lane. If that horse panics and decides to stop, you are going to have a real wreck among the horses following. It is at a time like that when the jockey will go to a hard whip to keep the horse motivated to move forward.

We normally don't have our exercise riders carry sticks, unless they're on a horse that is inclined to see something scary, stop and back up.

The key person in your pre-race dealings with a jockey is his agent. That person's prime goal is to get their client on horses that will win because that is how they both make money. The jockey gets a percentage of what the horse wins and the agent gets a percentage of what the jockey earns.

It is almost as important for a trainer to get to know and understand a jockey's agent as it is the jockey himself. Deal with those you can trust and avoid those who will give you whatever song and dance they think is required to get a mount from you that they think can win, but who won't remember your name down the road when they're romancing the trainer of what they've decided is a better horse.

Good horses make good jockeys more often than good jockeys make good horses. It is hard at times to sit in the stands beside an owner who is asking you why so and so who wins only about once in every 15 outs is on your horse and the meet's leading jockey is on the favorite. The thing you must try to explain and understand yourself is that it's kind of a chicken and egg proposition. Which comes first? True, that jockey might be the meet's leading rider, but it also might be true that he holds that position because he has consistently gotten the call on the best horses.

Look what happens to many young apprentices. When they first start riding, they are given a five-pound weight advantage. This means that if the lightest weight for a journeyman jockey is 117 pounds in a particular race, the apprentice or "bug boy" can carry 112.

Because of this, a lot of trainers will put apprentices on

their best horses, just to get the weight advantage. The apprentice becomes a sensation, winning race after race.

However, once the "bug" advantage is lost and the apprentice is no longer an apprentice and must meet the same weight requirements as everyone else, the good horses stop coming his way and his career nose-dives.

It is also good to remember that jockeys aren't miracle workers. Like the trainer, the jockey isn't going to be any better than the horse he rides. He or she can be the greatest rider in the world, but if they are riding an inferior horse in a tough field, they are normally going to lose.

On the other hand, good jockeys, like the class horses will find a way to win when everything else is equal. Put a good jockey and one with average ability astride two horses with the same ability and the good jockey will find a way to cross the finish line first.

When I say you want to find a jockey who will work with you, not just for you, it goes beyond just race day. If you have a stakes quality horse, you are going to want a jockey who is willing to come out to the track during early morning training sessions and work the horse and help you with the fine tuning before a major race.

We have discussed at length the training that goes into developing a horse and the people involved. Now, it's time to take a look at the equipment we use in training and racing.

Chapter 18

Equipment , Feeding and Drugs

Any trainer or would-be trainer who reads this chapter and expects to learn some deep, dark secrets about equipment, feeding or drugs that will make horses run faster is going to be disappointed. I have yet to find a piece of equipment, a particular food supply or drug that will make a horse run faster than it's genetically capable of doing.

Instead, the reverse is more often true. If you don't feed properly, use the correct equipment and offer appropriate therapeutic help, you can compromise a horse's ability.

Often in a training barn, when a horse turns in a sub-par performance, the topic of conversation becomes equipment. Next time, the trainer may declare, we'll run him in this or that kind of bit or whatever and he's sure to do better.

Let me, in advance, sum up my feelings about much of the exotic equine equipment being used today with a personal story of an incident when I was a high school kid. A good friend of the family ran a sporting goods store with the emphasis on hunting and fishing. I was planning to go fishing and went in there to buy some equipment.

As I looked at the thousands of hooks and lures spread out before me in tantalizing fashion, I was confused and asked my friend to help me out.

He smiled as he saw me staring in confusion at all of the fancy, brightly painted lures.

"Carl," he said, "most of these lures are designed to catch fishermen, not fish."

It is the same in the horse world. There is always going to be that unique horse that will need a unique bit, special set of shoes or one-of-a-kind blinker, but most of the exotic equipment and supplements offered on the market today is designed to catch horsemen, not to help the horse.

If you decide to change equipment on your horse, you should first ask yourself why, and what you expect to accomplish from this change. If you don't have logical, clear-cut answers to those questions, you must face the fact that you are making the change for no valid reason. You are perhaps succumbing, like the fishermen alluded to by my friend, to the latest fad that someone has declared can make your horse a winner.

Rather than constantly changing equipment in an effort to solve a problem, let's try to figure out why the horse is reacting the way it is. Have we adjusted as we should to the horse's needs?

If a horse is bearing out, for example, it is far better to learn why and seek to solve the problem rather than fit the animal with a severe runout bit which merely treats the symptom and does nothing to solve the problem.

Basic Bits

When it comes to bits, by the way, I'm about as basic as you can get. If you look through our tack room, the bit you will find that is being used as a routine piece of equipment is a jointed snaffle with large round rings.

I know there are dozens of bits on the market that are designed to solve or correct about every problem known to man. Nearly all of them, however, do nothing to get at the root of the problem - they only deal with the symptoms.

In an earlier chapter I mentioned a filly that began to bear out severely during a morning training session. If we had put a severe bit on her to solve the problem, we may have been able to keep her in line, but we also may never have found that the real problem involved her breathing apparatus. And, if we had merely treated the symptom we'd have been teaching this filly to cheat because the slower she traveled, the less air she'd need.

The basic purposes of a bit are to stop and turn a horse. In my opinion, nothing transcends the simple snaffle for these purposes. There is the occasional need for a more severe bit, but there isn't a bit manufactured that will permit a 120 pound person to stop or turn a 1,200 pound horse if the animal sets its mind to running off.

If you're having trouble controlling a horse with the snaffle and switch to a more severe bit without seeking out the source of the problem, it will be just a matter of time before the horse becomes hardened to the pressure brought to bear by that bit and then you'll have to get one that's even more severe. Eventually you will have run the entire gamut of severe bits without being able to control the horse or having a clue as to the root cause.

Using Blinkers

One piece of equipment that I have found useful in varying degrees is a set of blinkers.

The prime purpose of any set of blinkers is to get the horse to focus on what it is doing in competition. Blinkers can also be helpful in relaxing a horse in a race.

Blinkers come in varied sizes and shapes to accomplish various purposes. Earlier I mentioned that we used an Australian blinker on the gelding, Rut, whose left eye problem caused him to jump shadows. The Australian blinker covers the entire eye with a screen-like material. It enables the horse to see well enough, but helps to soften or obliterate shadows and cut down on sun glare. With Rut, we taped the bottom of the left Australian blinker so he couldn't see shadows on the ground at all.

An Australian Blinker covers the entire eye with a screen-like material to eliminate shadows but does not interfere with the horse's vision.
Photo by Caren Goodrich

The full cup blinker is the most restrictive to the horse's vision. It permits the horse to look straight ahead with tunnel vision, but it can't see to either the left or right. The prime purpose of this type of blinker is to force the horse to concentrate only on the track ahead. In my experience, very few horses have needed this type of blinker. I feel that if a horse is in such a fragile mental state that it can't handle seeing other horses on either side, its racing ability already has been compromised.

A blinker that I have found valuable is the runout blinker. This is a blinker that's affixed over the right eye. I have found this blinker to be far more effective than a runout bit for horses that tend to carry wide, particularly around turns. The reasons for bearing out can be many. The first step is to attempt to figure out why the horse is bearing out and take steps to correct the root problem.

Sometimes blinkers can be a part of the solution. Perhaps the horse isn't switching leads and is getting tired. As it tires, it drifts away in an effort to alleviate strain on the leading leg. By using the runout blinker, we take away peripheral vision to the right, convincing the horse to stay on course because it isn't going to run where it can't see.

Once we have the horse staying where it belongs, the rider can help solve the lead change problem.

Sometimes, you will get a horse that bears out as the result of an earlier bad experience that you may not know about and are unable to overcome. Here, again, I prefer the runout blinker over a severe bit because you are doing nothing to inhibit the horse's forward motion; you are merely cutting down its range of vision, which will tend to keep it on course.

When a horse watches the rider in a race, it can cause it to lose proper concentration. I want a horse running along free and easy, not tensing up and trying to anticipate what the jockey is doing.

To prevent this I use the short or "cheater" blinkers. The blinkers jut out about one inch from the hood over each eye. They don't really inhibit vision; they are just out there far enough so the horse can't see behind to clock the rider.

I have also had success with the three-quarter cup which restricts vision a bit more than the "cheaters" . Again, the equipment's prime purpose is to get the horse to focus on the job at hand and not allow it to concentrate on the horses to the right or left. It's also helpful for horses that have a habit of bearing in or out. Remember, a horse isn't going to go anywhere it can't see unless it's one scared sonofagun.

With some horses, blinkers have a compromising rather

229

than beneficial effect. Unbridled won his first race and lost his second. I thought maybe he needed blinkers so I tried him with a set. It was almost laughable. This horse was so curious that he kept trying to turn his head around to see what was happening beyond that limited field of vision.

I removed the blinkers before we were away from the barn and he never wore them again. Unbridled loved seeing everything that was going on around him.

Shoeing

When it comes to shoeing, I'm about as basic as with bits. Horses in the stable wear aluminum racing plates that are formed to fit the foot. It is abnormal for a horse to wear shoes, so I want the shoes to be as unobtrusive as possible. However, while it's abnormal for a horse to wear shoes, it's also abnormal for a horse to be walking over rocks and concrete, which our racehorses must do. Shoes protect the hooves from these hard surfaces. A sore-footed horse can't run.

Most of my runners will be shod with low toe grabs. I don't want to inhibit the action of the foot in sliding forward when it first strikes the surface, but I do want to aid it in getting a good hold when pushing off.

It may have sounded a little too basic when I said the shoes my horses wear are formed to fit the hoof. To me that's a must. Too often we ask farriers to trim or shoe a foot this way or that in an effort to change the way in which it strikes the ground. I firmly believe that by doing this, in most instances, you are begging for soundness problems.

If a horse is born with a particular alignment of its leg and foot bones, tendons and ligaments, there is no positive change in that alignment that man can effect after the animal reaches the track. If, for example, we attempt to straighten a turned out foot with shoeing, we render the horse incapable of properly absorbing concussion. Instead, undue stress is placed on bones and the supporting system because they have been forced out of their natural alignment and soundness problems are inevitable.

Trim and shoe the foot to its natural conformation.

There are, however, certain steps a farrier can take in shoeing to prevent a horse from overreaching or perhaps interfering behind.

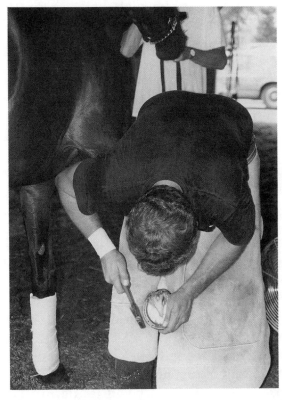

Horses in the stable are shod with aluminum racing plates formed to fit the foot.
Photo by Les Sellnow

Farrier work is a science unto itself and a trainer should make certain that his blacksmith knows and understands equine anatomy. The blacksmith is an integral part of the overall race team.

Feeding the Horse

Horse feed is a science, but feeding horses is an art.

There are tons of supplements and equine dietary aids on the market today. What a trainer has to determine is which of these aids are truly helpful in the overall nutritional package.

Nowhere are there more fads than in horse supplements. Somebody gives a testimonial that he won 10 races in a row while feeding Brand X and everybody feeds it. They don't win 10 races in a row as a result, so pretty soon they're switching to something else.

My advice to any trainer is to work closely with a nutritionist. There have been more changes in equine nutrition in the past five years than there were in the preceding 20; far more information than the average layman can cope. Align yourself with a nutritionist and make certain that the feed and supplements you are feeding are fresh and that they contain the ingredients you are seeking.

I want to know everything my feed contains and I want it to be fresh and of the highest quality. I want my supplements mixed within 30 days of the time I receive shipment; not having gathered dust through summer' heat and winter's cold in some feed company's warehouse.

The basic grains we feed are oats and barley. I buy the best oats and barley available on the market. To make it more palatable, the barley is crimped.

I consider barley a high-energy food. As the training regimen demands more energy from a horse, the barley portion of the ration is increased. If a horse is being let down, the reverse is true - less barley.

The hay that is in front of the horses nearly around the clock is a high quality timothy or, if it isn't available, orchard grass. In addition, each horse receives a block of rich, clean alfalfa hay each day.

232

Each horse is fed on an individual basis. Each has its individual feed card which calls for a specific ration to meet its specific needs.

As I mentioned earlier, I feed twice a day. The first feeding is given when training is finished in the morning and the second is given in the evening. To reiterate, the reason is to allow each horse all the time it needs to consume its particular ration.

The hay that is front of the horses nearly around the clock is high-quality timothy.

Photo by Les Sellnow

We have some horses in the barn that won't clean up their evening feeding until 2 or 3 a.m. the next day. They will eat a small amount, lie down and take a nap, get up and eat some more. If we attempted to get them to eat within a specific, short time frame, they wouldn't be getting the nutrition they need.

I think the best method would be to feed small amounts of feed four times a day, but shedrow routine makes that

233

difficult. My compromise is to feed twice, but to give them all the time they need to clean it up.

We also provide salt blocks on a free choice basis.

I repeat, horse feed is a science but feeding a horse is an art.

Drugs and Medication

Drugs have been more detrimental to the image of Thoroughbreds and racing in the public mind than anything else. Millions of dollars have been spent by certain elements within the racing industry to prove that Lasix (furosomide) hops up horses. The effect has been an eroding of the public's confidence in the integrity of racing. If only a portion of that money had been spent to educate the race-going public that Lasix is a diuretic that can be beneficial in preventing bleeding (exercise induced pulmonary hemorrhage), racing would have been the benefactor.

Lasix is not a stimulant, it is a diuretic. The only reason Lasix was restricted was, being a diuretic, it has the potential to mask illegal drugs. Our testing procedures in the last ten years have advanced to a point where this is not a factor.

Many race-goers are convinced that phenylbutazone (Bute) is a narcotic and as such is harmful to the horse. It is neither. Bute is an anti-inflammatory agent, not a pain killer as such.

Believe me, if a horse has a chip in its knee, you can give it all the Bute you want and it's still going to be lame. Yet, it can be very beneficial if, for example, a horse has a little muscle soreness, just as you or I might when we exercise.

The horse, if untreated, will tend to favor the sore side and may shift weight to the other leg to a degree that it will damage the sound leg. If the same horse had been treated with Bute, it likely would have worked through the temporary

234

soreness without compromising the other limb.

Horses are athletes and should be treated as such.

Contrary to what many in the public sector might think, no responsible trainer wants to be running against a horse that has been "shot up" with a pain killing substance to get one more race over legs that are threatening to break down. When that breakdown occurs the life of every horse and every jockey on the track is placed at risk.

Even if you find a way to mask pain with a drug you are not able to get past the test barn, which is highly unlikely with the scientific methods employed today, it will accomplish little in the long run. What happens to people who are hooked on drugs? Their whole body quickly deteriorates. A horse is no different. Drugs cause a deterioration of the animal's entire physical and nervous system.

Just like with people, drugs can be a horse's worst enemy.

Anytime you rely on something that is destructive to a horse's system, you are effectively shortening that animal's career.

Neither Lasix nor Bute fit into that category. They are useful medications that can aid and prolong a horse's athletic life. Of course, overuse of anything is detrimental. Aspirin is considered very useful for a number of problems. Yet, if you took 100 aspirins a day, a useful product would quickly become a harmful one.

So much for equipment, feed and drugs. Let's talk about shipping our racehorses cross country.

Chapter 19

Shipping Cross Country

The airplane makes it possible to ship horses anywhere in this country and even around the world for races. That's the upside. The downside is that shipping by air is expensive.

Because of the expense, one should pick and choose carefully which horses to ship and where. This is where good planning is necessary. When you have a horse that is developing into a major stakes contender, or at least shows that potential, make some long-range plans as to where you will run and when, as we did for Unbridled after setting our sights on the Kentucky Derby. When you establish a long-range plan, you not only are setting a blueprint for training, but also are able to pretty well define what the expenses will be for the campaign.

Because of the cost of air shipping and related expenses, plus entry fee, it is a rule of thumb that you have to finish at least third in a stakes race to break even financially when shipping

Does shipping long distances take something out of a horse physically? With some horses, yes, and with others, no. It depends on the horse and on the circumstances involved in the trip.

I think we can use human experiences as a valid comparison. Let us assume you have been preparing for a ski trip to Aspen and you planned and saved to do it first class.

You want a nice car to drive from the Denver airport to the ski lodge. Once there, you want a quiet candlelight dinner with your wife. And after dinner, you want to retire to a picturesque lodge for an evening of rest so you can hit the slopes early the next morning.

Everything goes well. Your flight is smooth and uninterrupted; your luggage is waiting for you in the baggage claim area, the car rental company has a new Cadillac standing by, the drive up the mountain through lightly falling snow is spectacular, your lodge is everything you wanted and more with a welcoming fire glowing in the fireplace and dinner is superb. The next morning you're going to be brimming with energy and will want to be on the slopes for a full day of exciting skiing.

Now turn that entire scenario around. You get on the plane, only to find it has mechanical problems. Finally, after deplaning and sitting in the terminal for hours, you get on another plane, only instead of a direct flight, you're routed through Detroit, where there's another delay. Late at night, you finally land in Denver. They can't find your luggage. It's somewhere in the skies on another plane. The car rental company has written you off and instead of a Cadillac, all they have left is a compact car. Whomever rented it before was a chain smoker and had spilled a can of beer in the back seat. It reeks of stale smoke and booze. You arrive at the ski resort with no hope of getting anything to eat. They also have written you off and rented your nice lodge to someone else. They manage to locate temporary accommodations for the rest of what will be a brief night, but warn you not to unpack because you will be moving in the morning.

Are you going to be in the mood to be up and at 'em the next day? I don't think so.

The same holds true for a horse. Let's assume it has a flight that gets delayed or rerouted and when the horse finally arrives at the track, the van is held up because the security man at the gate doesn't have the right paper work. Finally, the horse is allowed on the grounds, only to find there's been a miscommunication and no stall with fresh water and food awaits. When all of these problems are solved at last, the horse is unloaded. By now, it is anxious and out of sorts, its normal routine or rhythm totally destroyed.

If you've allowed only a day or two between arrival and the race, you might have trouble getting this horse focused on the task at hand - winning a race.

For most cross-country shipping to a stakes race, I like to arrive one day, walk and gallop the next, jog on the following morning and race that afternoon.

When shipping to a major event where there is much more activity, stress and pressure, such as Breeders' Cup, and where you want to get a work in over the track, I try to arrive at least 10 days ahead of time. In my opinion, you should either arrive and race within two or three days or else arrive at least 10 days in advance.

Much of my reasoning for the above involves the horse's mental response to shipping. If it doesn't mind travel and if you have been fortunate to have had a successful race after its first trip, the horse is going to equate travel with excitement and success. Thus, when you ship the horse it gets on an adrenaline high. If you race shortly after arriving, the horse is still on that high and likely will put forth its very best effort.

Again, we can use our ski trip for comparison. We know when starting the trip that skiing is what we're going to do and what we want to do. When we arrive, we are all keyed up and excited about getting to the slopes. If our vacation is extended, some of that excitement will dissipate and we will approach our fun with less intensity.

If we want to spend some time at a track to be certain the horse is comfortable with the surface, we will need the 10

239

days to let it come down from that first high, relax as it accepts the new surroundings as home, and then build to a second high by the time race day rolls around. We will induce that second high, perhaps with a sharp work after the horse has first relaxed and settled in at the track with walks, jogs and gallops.

Unbridled was a horse that loved to travel. You could just feel the excitement build in him when he was being led to an airplane or van. While I was happy that travel suited him, I also wanted his surroundings in a strange place to be as familiar as possible.

The airplane makes it possible to take advantage of stakes races anywhere in the world. Due to the expense, pick and choose carefully which horses to ship and which races to run.

His regular groom always traveled with him, either in the van or on the plane and was there on the lead shank when it came time to deplane or unload from the van. His stall would be prepared just like it was back at the home barn.

With Unbridled, we took it an additional step. There

240

was a pony we used regularly that he really liked, so wherever Unbridled went, the pony went. An incident that emphasized to us the value of a traveling companion occurred in a strange stable shortly after arrival. Unbridled was in one stall, the pony was in the one next to him. After being released in the enclosure, Unbridled took a turn or two around the stall, came to the door and stretched out his head and neck toward the pony. The pony did the same thing in his stall and they stood there a moment touching noses.

Satisfied that his security blanket was in place, Unbridled turned to his hay net and began eating, completely relaxed in the new environment.

To some degree, you lose a home field advantage for both horse and jockey when you ship, though modern-day jet service has helped negate that problem. In the old days, jockeys pretty much moved their tack to one part of the country and stayed there. Today, it's not unusual for a jockey to be riding in California one day and in New York the next.

This means that the leading jockeys pretty much have a handle on all the major tracks around the country. Chris McCarron may headquarter in California, for example, but he's also familiar with Belmont Park and Aqueduct in New York.

While you may not lose significant advantage from the jockey point of view when shipping, you must be aware that each track surface is different. Some are traditionally deep and slow, others are hard and fast. Again, it is a matter of knowing your horse and what type of surface it favors.

If you have a come-from-behind horse and are pointing toward a particular race, but know that the track has a strong speed bias and the horses likely to be entered are all speed horses, you might want to weigh that decision carefully.

We faced that problem with Unbridled going into the Preakness. We were committed to trying for the Triple Crown, but we knew that Pimlico is a track that favors speed horses.

This meant that conditions would be more to the liking of a tactical speed horse like Summer Squall than a come from behind runner like Unbridled. It was just the reverse from Churchill Downs where the track surface was perfect for Unbridled, but tended to take some of the edge off a speed horse.

As it turned out, the track at Pimlico, though still favoring speed, wasn't unduly tight for the Preakness. Still, it was Summer Squall's race. It set up just right for him because of the surface and because we were forced to move a little too early.

That's horse racing. Unbridled gave it his best shot and came up a little short in the Preakness.

Unfortunately, not all tracks are well maintained. There are some awful tracks out there and they stay that way because trainers do not have any control over surface conditions. Their only recourse is to refuse to run on a particular surface if they fear its consequences. Often, that is easier said than done when a particular track is offering just the race your horse needs as part of its planned campaign.

I believe that the ideal track is one that allows class to win a horse race. This means it isn't biased toward speed and it isn't biased in favor of horses with a late kick. It's somewhere in between; a track where speed can hold up if the front runner is a class horse and also a track where a horse can come from off the pace and win if it has the class to close.

How do you know if a track is speed biased? Easy. Just walk out there and stomp down hard with your foot. If it is tightened for speed, you will feel the shock waves travel up your leg. If you can feel the jolt just from stomping, think what it's like for a horse running at speed with, at one point in each stride, all of its weight slamming down on a fragile foreleg.

You also know it is speed biased when race after race, the three horses on the lead at the quarter pole, finish one, two, three. Conversely, you know the track is too heavy when race after race, the three front runners run out of steam at the quarter pole and finish at the back of the pack.

When you are on a track that is either too hard or too giving, the jockey becomes a more important element. Each track will have lanes where the surface will vary in tightness. After riding a couple preliminary races over a track, a jockey will know where those lanes are. If you, as the trainer, have communicated to him which surface your horse favors, the good jockey will find the lane that most suits it and will keep the horse there through most of the race.

Class should decide a horse race, not the track surface.

While you try to keep everything as normal as possible for your horse when shipping, some things, in addition to track surfaces, are out of your control. Hay, grain and straw fit into this category. If you're shipping by air, it is all but impossible to carry all your feed with you. You must try to buy hay, grain and straw at the new location that approximates what the horse is used to having.

There is also the question of when to feed after you have passed through a few time zones. If you are going from Eastern to Pacific time or vice versa, for example, the difference is three hours. Because one must adapt to the different time zone as far as training hours are concerned, I try to at least compromise on feeding times. When it's noon in California, it's already 3 p.m. in Kentucky or New York. Rather than keep the horse on an Eastern Time feeding schedule, I'll try to feed at a time that's somewhere between the two.

When arriving at a new location or returning home after shipping, we will normally cut back on the horse's ration for the first feeding or two after arrival. The first day at a new location or after returning home, we will normally walk around the shedrow to get the horse acclimated and then proceed with the pre-planned training schedule the following day.

A new location also means new personnel. If you want the horse 'scoped, for example, the vet doing it will be a strange presence for the horse as will the blacksmith if you have shoeing problems. If the horse you ship has a problem with the gate, you must be aware that you will be dealing with a strange gate crew.

Then, too, there is the matter of at least a slight degree of home field advantage for jockeys who ride a track on a daily basis. While it's true, as I said earlier, that jockeys routinely travel around the country to ride in major races, they can never get to know a track as thoroughly as a jockey who rides on it every day. Each track will have its own quirks and peculiarities, depending on weather conditions. Only a jockey who rides on it regularly will know what to expect when it's raining or, on the other hand, when the day is hot and dry.

A major factor involved in the shipping decision is whether your horse is on an upswing or a downswing. If the horse is training well and running well in competition, shipping should be no problem.

If, on the other hand, the horse has had a problem race or two and has responded to stress by becoming nervous and anxious around the barn and during training sessions, shipping may only aggravate the problem.

The same is true with success or failure at the track to which you ship. You might ship a horse to a particular track with the horse handling it well, but for one reason or another, it has a horrible race. That could have a profound effect on how that horse ships the next time. Normally, a horse doesn't become stressed from being loaded onto a van or plane. The stress will come from fearing what will happen when it gets there. Horses are adept at remembering bad experiences.

Some horses are claustrophobic. They panic when locked into tight quarters. When that's the case, you must make certain they have plenty of space in the van and that the groom they know and trust is at hand to instill confidence.

Shipping short distances by van normally doesn't present problems; such as stabling at Churchill Downs and shipping to Lexington, some 70 miles away, for a race.

Even for short trips, however, we handle our horses the same as if we were traveling a long distance across the country. The groom will be back there in the van and upon arrival the horse will go into a stall that's prepared just like the one at the home track. The comfort factor and lack of stress make a big difference.

The horse that makes even a short trip in a spacious van normally will show no effects, other than perhaps heightened anticipation, which is positive. However, if the horse is loaded into a small trailer, buzzing with flies and the driver decides to park in the hot sun while he stops for lunch, the horse can arrive at its destination thoroughly stressed.

On the positive side, as I have already alluded to, shipping signals the horse that a race is imminent and that can be an advantage because of the adrenaline high. I have had horses get all focused and ready to run when you approach with bridle or saddle in new surroundings.

The key element, as with everything else we have discussed to this point, is the trainer's ability to adjust to what the horse needs and wants. If it loves to travel, wonderful. If it doesn't and you feel you have to ship to certain races, do everything possible to negate the stress. Your goal is to get the same type of performance, or better, from the horse as you would at the home track.

Now that we have discussed shipping, let us turn our attention to what is involved in entering a race either at the home track or somewhere else.

Chapter 20

Dealing With Track Officials

One of the most important persons with whom a trainer will deal on the racetrack is the racing secretary. It is the responsibility of the racing secretary to set conditions for each race and also to assign weight in those races where it varies from horse to horse.

A good racing secretary will be familiar with the horses stabled at his track. He will know how many two-year-olds, three-year-olds and older horses are on hand to form the pool which will fill the races he writes for each day's program.

At some tracks, especially the major ones, the secretary will have established a pattern or rhythm that will, generally speaking, hold true meet after meet. When that's the case, it's relatively easy for the trainer to dovetail his or her own long-range plans with the races offered.

The specific conditions for each race day are set forth in a conditions book issued by the racing secretary's office. The conditions book lists races to be run 10 days to two weeks in the future. Each trainer gets a copy of the conditions book so he or she can look into the future and decide which horses to run and when.

It behooves a trainer to know and understand the pattern or rhythm of the racing secretary at the track where he or she is located. For example, you might have a three-year-old that needs a certain type of race. You look at the conditions book and it isn't there. If you know how the racing secretary operates, that may not be cause for concern as you know, based on past experience, that he will include the race in the next conditions book. This means you can sharpen your horse with that race in mind, even though it hasn't yet been written.

Racing secretaries aren't always the most popular persons among trainers. You might look at a certain conditions book and find there is very little that fits you. Immediately, your inclination is to blame the racing secretary for being short-sighted. What you must always keep in mind is that the racing secretary can't concern himself with one trainer; he must write races that will benefit the majority.

When a trainer arrives at a track with his stable, he lets the racing secretary know which horses are on the grounds. Again, computers help to ease the burden for everyone. The racing secretary can call up the racing records, as kept by the Jockey Club, on every horse present. They will know how many sprinters are there as well as how many distance horses; how many will run on dirt and how many only on turf.

They also have a handle on how often trainers run their horses. If there is a stakes race on the calendar, they may write in an allowance race as a prep for it several weeks before the stakes. A good racing secretary will do everything he can to accommodate the horses and trainers at his track.

As with trainers, the racing secretary faces certain problems over which he has no control. He might write a race that should have a dozen good horses entering, only to have rain on race day turn the track into a quagmire. Half of those entries might scratch because the trainers don't want their horses running in mud.

Entries for race day, generally speaking, are taken 48 hours ahead of time. The trainer or assistant trainer goes to the secretary's office and makes the entry.

Official Starter

A person that can make or break a race is the official starter. It is his job to get the horses out of the gate in good order so that each one starts on equal footing. Starters and their techniques vary and it is up to the trainer and the jockey to know their rhythm. Some are quick. The door is hardly slamming shut on the last horse when the electronic gates swing open in front and they're off. Others are more inclined to wait longer, making certain each horse is correctly positioned.

The hope is that when the gates fly open, each horse is standing four square and alert, ready to burst forth running. Under the best of conditions this is a difficult goal to meet. Think of all the major stakes races you've seen on television where horses slam into each other coming out of the gate.

Working with the official starter is a gate crew or assistant starters and a driver who pilots the tractor or, in some cases, the horses which pull the starting gate. Proper positioning of the gate is highly important.

It's imperative that the driver know the course like the palm of his hand. To set the gate at the three-quarter pole may seem easy to the fan in the stands, until you realize that even the slightest of angles could send the field either into the outer or inner rail.

Conversely, the configuration of the track at Belmont Park dictates that the gate be set at an angle for mile and one-quarter races in order to get everyone off on line and running down the track instead of into the rails.

The assistant starters have the responsibility of getting the horses into the starting gate and, once there, helping the jockeys steady them. Sometimes the only way they can force a reluctant horse into the gate is to lock arms behind its rump and push it forward. Believe me, this is not the safest position in which to be.

Once the horse is in the gate, the assistant starter

climbs up beside the horse's head. If that animal goes to rearing and plunging, the assistant starter may find himself in a precarious and dangerous situation. In addition to helping quiet the horse in the gate, the assistant starter will attempt to keep the horse's head straight, so when the gate opens, the horse is looking down the track instead of to one side or the other.

The assistant starters have a major responsibility in loading the horses into the gate and keeping them calm for the start. *Photo by Les Sellnow*

It is also their job to notify the starter if something is awry, such as a horse leaning against a side wall or sitting on its haunches. If a delay is needed to remedy the situation, the assistant starter must so inform the starter.

The assistant starter will also keep the jockey with whom he's working apprised of what's happening with the rest of the field that's being loaded: "Two back - now one back - they're all in."

The starter, atop an elevated stand in front, and off to the side of the gate is watching and listening to everything, sometimes spotting a problem that the assistants failed to see. He wants to get the horses out of that gate as quickly as possible, once they are all loaded because the longer these fired up balls of energy and nerves are forced to remain in the gate, the greater the potential for problems.

A quick glance across the gate. They're all in line,

The gates fly open as one. The horses blast forward and the race is on!
Photo by Suzie Oldham

looking forward. He presses the button. The gates fly open as one. The horses blast forward and the race is on.

There is no time for the starting crew to become spectators. The starter cable is rolled up and the driver moves the gate. If the horses are to pass over the starting spot on the way to the finish line, the assistants grab rakes and quickly smooth over the tracks left by the tractor and the gate and then head for the next race's starting point.

The Outrider

The unsung hero at every track during both training and racing sessions is the outrider. This is a person who frequently must suffer verbal abuse while rarely getting praise. If a horse gets free and goes careening down the track, it's the outrider's job to catch it. If he does, he' a brief hero, though it's what is expected of him. If he misses, he's vilified.

The outrider is the on-track officer in charge during training and racing sessions. He is equipped during the race with a radio that allows him to have instant contact with security and the stewards. At a track like Arlington International Racecourse where training begins at 5:30 a.m., it is the outrider who gives the official word to open the gates so horses can enter the track.

From that point on, he serves as a traffic policeman who enforces track rules. Sometimes, as mentioned, he must become a one-person posse as he moves into position to stop a runaway that has pitched its rider. It is also his responsibility to make certain that ambulances are in position and staffed - one for humans and one for horses.

As training proceeds of a morning, the outrider, aboard his steady steed, will cruise the track, his eyes ever mindful for paper and other debris that might make an unwelcome appearance on a windy day and spook a horse.

It takes skill and excellent horsemanship for an outrider to intercept and stop a runaway. Being successful or unsuccessful in stopping a runaway can make the difference between the incident being minor or major. When it is major, it can result in serious injury to both horses and humans.

When minor, it is quickly forgotten as just another little incident in a training morning.

Success or failure in stopping a runaway can rest with calculating the correct angle at which to approach and knowing instinctively at what speed. If the outrider comes in at too sharp an angle and with too much speed, the runaway may duck back behind the catch pony. If he comes in at too slight an angle and not fast enough, his pony may not be able to catch up and the runaway will continue on its merry way, posing a hazard to itself, other riders and their mounts.

The outrider remains on duty all through training hours, sometimes switching to a fresh horse if it's been a particularly hectic day. When the track closes for the morning, he takes a break, but reports back on duty before the afternoon's program. In the afternoon, there will be two outriders, one in the front and one in the rear of the post parade.

The outrider in front is responsible for leading the post parade and bringing the horses to the post on time. He also will be the outrider who positions himself in front of the gate, and off to one side, while the horses are being loaded. He is on guard in case one of the runners breaks through the front barrier before the starter hits the button to open the gates.

The rear outrider is to assist any horse that has difficulties in the post parade and to make certain the runners are in numerical order when they reach the starting gate at post time. This outrider remains behind the gate to catch any horse that might escape the starting gate to the rear.

The outrider's day ends when the final race has been run and all horses are back in their stalls. Before 5 a.m. the next day, he once again reports for duty.

Track Veterinarians

Important officials who are rarely seen by the racing

public are the track veterinarians. They are charged with the horses' safety and to make certain the track's rules on medication are adhered to.

If you want to run a horse on Lasix or Bute at a jurisdiction where those medications are approved, the track veterinarian must, at a specified time prior to the race, be so informed by the veterinarian who will administer the medication. If the track veterinarian is not so informed and the horse wins, but the drugs show up in the urine sample taken, the horse can be disqualified and the trainer will face serious penalty.

On the morning of race day at most jurisdictions, the track veterinarians will give a brief physical examination to each horse entered. They will be looking for heat in the legs as well as for puffiness or swelling. These are signs that a horse is suffering from an ailment that may compromise its ability to run effectively as well as its chances of running safely.

The vast majority of trainers would have detected the problem well in advance of race morning and scratched the horse, but there is that minority who will try to slip an unsound horse into a race in the hopes that it will either finish in the money or be claimed. It's the track veterinarian's responsibility to protect the horse against such unethical behavior.

An official veterinarian is also on the track to keep the horses under surveillance both before and after each race. If he sees a horse that appears unsound in the saddling paddock or post parade, he will immediately inform the stewards and the horse will be scratched.

The veterinarians also visually examine each horse after a race when it returns to be unsaddled. If a horse appears unsound, the track vet will record the information and will closely evaluate the horse before allowing it to start another race.

254

The track veterinarians and crew also are responsible for taking, labeling and submitting urine samples to designated laboratories for drug testing. Half of the sample is sent to the designated laboratory and half is maintained under lock and key for further testing at a neutral laboratory in case there is a positive finding for drugs.

Track Stewards

The most powerful behind the scenes person is the racetrack steward. His power extends from scratching horses in a race to affixing penalties against jockeys who violate the rules both on the track and off.

If a jockey is found to have ridden in a reckless manner in a race, the steward has the power to suspend him or her from competition for a period of time.

If a jockey has a problem with drugs, the steward can call for routine drug tests to determine whether the jockey is staying clean. If he violates regulations, the steward has the power to rule him off the track.

The steward also has the final authority as to whether a horse can start a race or be scratched. As I mentioned earlier, if the track veterinarian sees a soundness problem, he or she reports it immediately to the steward. If the steward agrees, as he normally will, the horse is scratched. There is no appealing the steward's decision at that point. If he says the horse is scratched, it's scratched.

There are a host of other behind the scenes workers that range from the person who checks the identification of each horse as it comes to the saddling paddock to the photographer who clicks the shutter on each photo finish.

There are two things that the above people have as a common goal if they are filling their jobs responsibly - the safety of the horses and protecting the integrity of racing.

Chapter 21

Becoming a Trainer

So you want to be a trainer.

It's a great way to make a living if you know, understand and love horses. However, that is not enough to insure success. A successful trainer must also be an astute businessman and public relations expert who has set goals for himself or herself and then worked unstintingly to reach them.

We've discussed at length the horsemanship aspect, which, I still believe is the most important ingredient. There are about as many approaches to training Thoroughbreds as there are trainers. However, there is one thing successful trainers have in common; they can tell you what a horse is doing, whether it's doing well or poorly, and, most importantly, they can tell you why. And, when a horse is doing poorly, the successful trainer will know how to adjust his training approach to open the door to improvement.

While training can be a complex exercise, so is survival in the business world outside the shedrow. You can be the best trainer in the world and still go broke if you don't handle your business affairs correctly and wisely. A trainer must have a good handle on all costs - from purchasing straw to paying workers' compensation and from vet bills to current interest rates.

Here again, computers have been a boon. By recording all data for each horse and each expense, we always know exactly what's being invested in the animal on a daily basis.

A trainer must also be a public relations expert. It is rare for an owner to stay with a trainer he or she doesn't like. Establishing a good working relationship between trainer and owner takes effort. I don't think a trainer has to fawn over his clients, but I do believe that he owes them an ongoing explanation of what's happening with their horses and a best guess estimate as what the future holds for them.

A trainer must always remember that without owners, he wouldn't have a job. They are the ones who put up the money to buy untried colts and fillies and they are the ones who pay the bills for training, vet work, shoeing, daily care and entry fees. Owners deserve to be apprised regularly on their horses' progress, be it good or bad.

They also deserve special attention on race day so they feel a part of the program. This includes accommodating them in the saddling paddock and being certain they get to the winner's circle for a celebratory photo when their horse crosses under the wire first.

It's also important for the trainer to know how to deal with the press if good fortune smiles and he comes up with the "big" horse. As I mentioned earlier, it is all but impossible to imagine the pressure publicity brings when you have a top horse. A trainer's every move is analyzed and questioned. How a trainer handles this kind of pressure is important to him, the horse, the owner and the general public.

I think a trainer's actions and words, when he or she is in the glare of publicity, should be such that they a create a positive image for racing in the public mind. It is, after all, our chosen way of life and we should do everything possible to enhance it.

Periodically, I'm asked what kind of background is required to become a horse trainer. There really is no answer to that question. Some successful trainers grew up on the backside because their dads were trainers. Others happened onto the scene accidentally, coming from varied backgrounds.

It doesn't really matter what your background is, so long as you have the ability to know and understand horses

Carl Nafzger and D. Wayne Lukas on the backstretch.
Photo by Dan Johnson

and can handle the pressures attendant to training and racing. You must be a person with a positive outlook and one who maintains an even keel when bouncing back and forth between the highs of exuberant triumphs and the lows of shattering defeats. Racing can take you to the pinnacle of success and drop you into the depths of despair, all in one day. It's the nature of the sport, and the people involved must have the fortitude to handle both with aplomb and dignity.

About the best way I can provide an insight into becoming a trainer and the trials, tribulations and pressures involved in the struggle to succeed, is to talk about my own emergence in the sport. I may not be typical, but then, I guess no one in racing is.

I was born in a little Texas town named Olton where my family was involved in farming and ranching. As I grew up, I had one burning desire - to be a rodeo cowboy. I can remember standing out in the cotton fields, watching planes go by overhead and wondering where they were going and what experiences might await one at their destination.

Rodeo, I was convinced, would give me those thrills and experiences.

When I was still in high school, we had about 60 bulls in a feedlot and I asked my dad if I could ride them for practice. We built a bucking chute and he helped me down on my first bull. I stayed aboard about two and one-half jumps out of the chute and then hit the ground with that bull running right over the top of me.

Rather than being discouraged, I knew right then that all I ever wanted to be was a bull rider.

I joined the Professional Rodeo Cowboys Association right after graduating from high school. I also attended college for a year, but that was put on hold so I could rodeo. I rodeoed hard in those days. In the beginning, I would be on the circuit 10 months of the year, learning and paying my dues; returning home in November and December to work in the cotton gin. Later as my skills improved and the prize money won increased, I would rodeo steady from Christmas through December 1 of the next year, taking only a few weeks off to recuperate from injuries and rest up.

By 1963 I was standing third in the world in bull riding and making a decent living from the sport. As the years went by, though, I realized that riding bulls as a steady diet was not something one should do for a permanent career. They kept running in fresh bulls, and I had to run in the same ol' battered body. I got into a major wreck on a bull in '66 and had to have a steel rod put in one leg. That forced me to take a time-out and to evaluate anew where I was going with my life.

By this time I'm in my late 20s and I realized that it was time to at least consider a different vocation for the future, so I went to horseshoeing school at Cal Poly Tech, thinking I might make my living as a farrier.

Though concentrating on rodeo at this stage of my life, I had always been fascinated by Thoroughbreds and racing. My first real experience with racing came about when my dad and I bought a cheap claimer named Ignoble down at Rilito Park in Tucson, Arizona. We put him with a trainer and he won his first race. We thought we were geniuses. We knew how to pick them.

In fact, we felt so good about him that we figured it was time for him to move up in class. The trainer agreed and took Ignoble to Ruidiso Downs in New Mexico. This was a major step upward in the level of competition.

I was on the rodeo circuit when he ran the first time in New Mexico. I drove all night after competing to get to the track in time to see him run. Feeling completely confident that Ignoble would do well, I bet my money on him.

Dad and I were sitting together in the grandstand for the race. Down the home stretch they came, Ignoble dead last.

Dad looked at me and said, "Carl, I think we bought us a roping horse."

"Roping horse?" I yelled back. "Roping horse? Hell, he couldn't even catch a calf."

"I don't know, he sure enough looks like a cattle horse to me," Dad said as they crossed under the wire, with Ignoble still the trailer.

"Cattle horse?" I asked. "What are you talking about?"

"Well," Dad said without cracking a smile, "did you watch him come down the lane? He didn't let a one of those horses turn back."

Despite Ignoble's setback when raced against class competition, I remained hooked. Though I kept rodeoing, I also kept a hand in racing. I bought part interest in a Thoroughbred mare. Later we bred her to a Quarter Horse stud and she had a nice colt that we named Royal Tonto. We - my dad and I and a couple friends - turned down $2,700 for him as a weanling. He was broke by a friend and won two races at Lubbock Downs.

It was time, we decided, to turn him over to a professional trainer. The horse had a club foot, but I had been doing the trimming and had managed to trim it in such a way that it didn't hinder him. I don't know what the trainer did or didn't do with this horse, but before long he was sore and couldn't run. My brother and I went down there and picked him up. For one thing, we discovered, they had trimmed the club foot all wrong and it looked like a stove pipe.

As we headed home, I told my brother, "I'm going to train racehorses."

My brother looked at me and asked, "What makes you think you can train them?"

"I don't know how good I can be at it," I replied, "but I know I can do better than the guy who's had our horse."

Wanda and I got married in the spring of '68. I had meant it when I said I was going to be a trainer, though I was off to a pretty humble start. Wanda and I headed to Ruidoso Downs that spring with one horse because we could only get one stall. To make ends meet, I shod pony horses, galloped for other trainers in the morning and ponied in the afternoons.

By the time August rolled around, our one horse had two fourths, a fifth and a sixth. We called the owner and said we were sending the horse back.

We were broke.

Wanda, who was a special education teacher, had been teaching school in Cheyenne, Wyoming, so off to Wyoming we went that fall. I got a job on the Polo Ranch where they raised Thoroughbreds and cattle. I spent my time shoeing horses, breaking them and, early each morning, feeding cattle.

I also rodeoed part-time.

When 1970 rolled around, I knew my rodeoing as an active participant was ending. I truly loved rodeo and wanted to stay with it, but no matter how I manipulated the figures, there wasn't enough money to be made.

It was decision time. "Wanda," I said over lunch one day, "let's train racehorses full-time." She was willing to try it.

I believe in setting goals, so we set a goal of owning 10 good broodmares and selling, training and racing their offspring. To get started, we had to have some money.

My dad and two brothers, Don and J.P., came up with $5,000. Wanda cashed in her school retirement fund which gave us another $3,500. So with $8,500 in our pockets we hooked a two-horse trailer behind the pickup and headed out of Texas for the Keeneland Sale in Lexington, Kentucky.

This would be my second visit to Keeneland. Earlier, in my rodeo days, a buddy and I passed through Lexington, traveling by car from North Carolina to a rodeo at the Cow Palace in San Francisco. When I saw the sign for Keeneland, I whipped in because I wanted to see the track.

"Curly," I said to my buddy as we drove slowly around, looking at the buildings and the track, "some day I'm going to race horses here."

Curly laughed. "Carl, they won't even let you in the gate."

The end of the story is that in 1977, we won our first race at Keeneland. I sent a copy of the win photo to Curly. We've remained good friends and Curly wound up investing in some Thoroughbreds.

But, that's getting ahead of myself. At our first buying venture at Keeneland, we decided that Don should be the pedigree man as he'd spent a lot of time learning about bloodlines. I was to be the guy who made the call on conformation. We would buy two fillies to begin building our broodmare band.

Our approach was straightforward and simple: we were going to buy the best horses we could afford. The main criteria was that they have good bloodlines and conformation and be sired by stallions who had earned at least $100,000 during their racing careers.

We bought a filly for $5,000 that filled the bill. Now, we were sitting on about $3,000 to buy a second one. This got tougher. Every yearling that met our criteria went beyond our price range. Finally, as the sale was winding down, a filly came through that we liked. Our last bid was our limit; $3,000. Down came the hammer and we owned her.

We loaded our two yearlings into the trailer and headed home to Texas. Halfway there, we stopped for the night and put the two fillies into a corral at the stock yards. The next day we loaded them again and finished the trip home.

While the two fillies were growing up, we converted an old Quonset hut into a nine-stall stable, doing all the work ourselves, and I hung out my shingle and started breaking horses. In the spring of '71 the man who owned the ranch in Wyoming sent a couple horses to me. We were in the training business with a total of six horses that were ready to run. I soon found out that sometimes it's who you know, not what you know that opens the right doors.

I applied for stalls at Santa Fe, only to be told none was available. I called the ranch owner in Wyoming to report the sad news. "Don't worry about it," he told me, "I know the racing secretary there. You'll have stalls."

He made a call and just that quickly, we had six stalls. It was a good meet. A filly in our stable set a track record the first time out. That was a definite high. When the meet ended, we were able to pay off the notes at the bank.

In the spring of 1972, I felt we had three horses that

were good enough to compete at Santa Anita so off to California we went. Of the three we took to Santa Anita, two did well and one was a washout.

A filly we called Pretty Little Bessie ran at the $10,000 claiming level. The other successful filly, named Malicious Scene, was doing well and I wound up selling her for $25,000. The new owner would take possession after one more race. The filly is leading at the head of the lane in that race when she injures an ankle. The sale was off. I was devastated. At that point in our lives, $25,000 was more money that Wanda and I had dreamed of.

The filly's ankle injury wasn't career ending, but she needed time to recuperate.

Each fall we would head back to Keeneland to buy more horses. Wanda kept groceries on the table with a teaching job in Olton.

Along the way we began having success with our runners and were steadily moving up in class. Racing as a family venture came to a halt in 1975 when my dad died. Wanda and I eventually bought out the other family members. Wanda kept teaching school to make ends meet and I kept training.

When people ask me who we tutored under, my reply is: "We learned under the best tutor in the world - our own time and money." I don't necessarily advise that approach to someone wanting to be a trainer today, but I will get into that a little later.

Learning by experience can bring some bitter, but not to be forgotten lessons. One of those bitter lessons involved listening to others and going against my own judgment. The year is 1976. Wanda is still teaching school and I managed to get some stalls at Oaklawn Park in Arkansas. I had a filly in training that we ran in a $20,000 allowance race. She was an unknown and went off at 60 to 1 odds with an apprentice jockey named Jerry Bailey aboard. She finished second and we had $4,000 in purse money. To Wanda and me, this was a fortune.

The surprise second place finish set the filly up for a stakes race. It seemed like everyone I talked to advised me to take young Jerry Bailey off the filly and replace him with a veteran jockey. I took their advice and that turned out to be a mistake I will always remember and one from which I learned a valuable lesson.

It was time for Wanda and me to set higher goals. We did. Our new goals included racing in the east. Wanda quit her teaching job and from 1977 on, we both devoted all of our time and energy to training and racing Thoroughbreds.

Carl and Wanda Nafzger after the 1990 Breeders' Cup Classic. *Photo by Leslie Martin*

Along the way, we had come to the attention of William Floyd and John Nerud of Tartan Farm. William Floyd owned Fairway Phantom, our big at the time. He won the Arlington

Classic in '81 and we took him to Saratoga for the Travers that summer.

It was at Saratoga that John Nerud asked if I would train Tartan Farm's Midwest string of racehorses. It didn't take us long to say yes. We were at Arlington Park with the Tartan string for the first time in 1982. At that time the Genter stable also decided to run a Midwest string.

Along the way we've had our share of ups, including a good many stakes winners and purses that have averaged out at about $1 million annually, and also our share of downs that have included injuries and horses that just simply didn't reach potential for one reason or another.

I tell the story of how Wanda and I got started in the business because it illustrates the fact that you don't have to have a certain background or set of experiences to get involved in racing as trainer or owner. When you come down to it, riding bulls and training Thoroughbreds have little in common other than respect for animals and the need to set goals and do your very best to reach them.

However, being on the rodeo circuit did prepare me for life as a Thoroughbred trainer in one other way. In rodeo, nobody guarantees you anything. You only earn what you are good enough to win. It is nothing like baseball or football where players get huge bonuses to sign and then are paid astronomical sums to continue playing.

As a rodeo contestant, you do your own scheduling, handle your finances, take care of your own transportation and are responsible for coming up with the money to pay your entry fees.

Being a racehorse trainer brings you no more financial guarantees than does rodeo. One day, you are living high with money to spare; the next day you are wondering how to pay your feed bills. You must learn to budget wisely, laying aside extra funds when you are flush so you have something to carry you through the inevitable bad times.

My advice to a would-be trainer today is to become involved with a class stable and work your way up. It would be to a person's advantage to start as a groom or hot walker. I don't mean you should stay in that position for years, but if you want to learn the ropes from the bottom up, that is the best place to start.

Your goal should be to attain the job of barn foreman. That is a great learning position because you must know your horses and you must be able to cope with people. In this role, you will observe horses on a daily basis and will learn what makes them tick. The experiences you have in dealing with grooms and hot walkers will provide the groundwork for future contact with both employees and owners.

After about two years as a barn foreman, you are ready to move up to assistant trainer. In this role you will assume more responsibility in preparing a horse for competition as you add exercise riders to the list of employees with whom you will work.

I also advise working in an area where you plan to locate once you get your trainer's license. If California is where you plan to train, then go to work for a California stable during your learning years. You will get to know other trainers, owners and officials in that area. Thus, when you get your license, everything and everybody will be familiar to you.

If you do your apprentice work in California and then move to New York, it's like starting all over because you won't be acquainted with any of the officials or trainers.

If you want to be a trainer, you must be person who not only can cope with pressure, but one who thrives on it. A photographer who covered action stories for a newspaper came up with a descriptive phrase for people who thrive on pressure.

We're all "adrenaline junkies," she said, hardly finishing one excitement or pressure high before we're looking for another.

Training racehorses can certainly give you the highs, but just as quickly it can deal you a low blow. The successful trainer is the person who can handle both.

There is no question that one of the greatest highs of my life was winning the Kentucky Derby with Unbridled. I promised earlier to tell the rest of that story and I'll keep my word.

Chapter 22

The Kentucky Derby

Much has been written and spoken concerning those dramatic moments at the Kentucky Derby when Unbridled unleashed a fantastic surge of power and speed to take the lead and win this country's most prestigious race.

Many horse racing fans will recall the finish of that race vividly. For sure, I do. Others will remember the emotional scene when I called the race for 92-year-old Frances Genter of Minnesota, the owner of Unbridled, and a wonderful lady who had been a staunch supporter of Thoroughbred breeding and racing for many years, but had never had a Derby winner.

I didn't know that my call of the race for Mrs. Genter was being filmed. Everything that happened that day was spontaneous - totally unplanned. The circumstances that led up to it began months before in the wake of the Florida Derby.

Mrs. Genter was present for that race and was thrilled with Unbridled's victory. Later we held a meeting in the Directors' Room at the track. It was then that I told Mrs. Genter, "We're going to go to the Kentucky Derby,"

"Well, Carl," she said, "that's good, but I won't be there because of the crowds. I'll probably be able to see it better at home on TV."

"No, Mrs. Genter," I said, "you're coming to the Kentucky Derby if I have to buy a TV and put it in the box in front of you."

She just smiled, but I knew she'd be there.

During the week before the Derby a reporter asked me, "How important is it for you to win the Kentucky Derby?"

"If I ever win a Kentucky Derby in my lifetime," I replied, "I want it to be this one because of Mrs. Genter."

A day or two before the Derby Mrs. Genter and members of her family flew to Kentucky. They stayed in Lexington and on Derby morning drove to Louisville.

It was a cold, cloudy day.

The folks at Churchill Downs were wonderful. They had us in a box with a television set located just in front of us for excellent viewing. The box was near the finish line and situated so no one could stand up in front of us and block our view. Because it was so cold, Mrs. Genter spent most of the day prior to the Derby itself in the Directors' Room where she could watch the races on TV and stay warm.

Earlier that day, Curt Gowdy Jr. of ABC television had asked if they could place a microphone on me so that commentator Jim McKay could ask for a comment either in the saddling paddock or during the post parade. I said, "You don't want to 'mike' me, I don't have one of the favorites in the race."

He replied that they were placing microphones on four trainers and he wanted me to be one of them. He said they would ask me just one question.

Along with the microphone was a small earphone that would enable me to listen to everything that was being said by the TV people before, during and after the race.

I agreed to wear the microphone.

Every once in a while I'd take the little earphone out of my overcoat pocket, place it in my ear and listen to what the commentators were saying.

The first time I put the earphone on, they were saying, it looked like Mr. Frisky's race because of all his wins.

I didn't need that so I took the earphone out and put it in my pocket.

A little later, I put it in again. This time, they were talking about Summer Squall and how he should be the favorite. No mention of Unbridled.

I took the earphone out again and put it in my pocket.

When it was time to saddle the horses, I put the earphone back in so that I would be ready to respond if called upon in the paddock. After saddling and giving jockey Craig Perret a leg up, we made our way to the box. On Derby day, this is no easy feat. Though Churchill Downs provides escorts to help get you through the crowd, it's still slow going because of the congestion. As big as Churchill is, the Derby fills it beyond normal capacity.

By the time we got to the box, they were playing *My Old Kentucky Home*. Mrs. Genter had left the Directors' Room and walked to the box. (A lot of people think she was wheelchair-bound, but she wasn't. She was taken to the winner's circle in a wheelchair after the race only because that was the fastest way to get there.)

At the verse in *My Old Kentucky Home* where it says. . ."The sun shines bright. . .," the sun came out. It shone directly on the TV set, making it impossible to see the images because of the glare.

At about the time the horses were approaching the starting gate, commentator Jim McKay came on and asked me what I thought about the wet track and whether it would pose a problem for Unbridled because he had a history of not liking off tracks.

I told him the track was no problem; that it would provide nobody with an excuse because the rain had stopped and the track surface was not slick.

When I finished with him, I took the earphone from my ear, put it in my pocket and forgot about it. As far as I was concerned that was the end of my being featured on television.

We faced a dilemma in the box. Where should we locate

Mrs. Genter so that she would able to follow the race's progress? It was a major problem because her eyesight was so poor she couldn't see the horses at the starting gate and would be able to follow the race only if she could see it on television. The glaring sunlight rendered the television set in front of our box useless.

I said she should stand beside me because I felt I would know better than anyone else just where Unbridled would be at each furlong marker.

I would call the race for her from start to finish.

When the horses left the starting gate and came past us the first time, I told her we were laying 10th or 11th, but that this was fine; it was right where we wanted to be. "He's running good," I told her.

I kept the field glasses on Unbridled as they rounded the turn and started down the backstretch. He was running smoothly and flawlessly.

At the half mile pole, Unbridled started to pass horses. "Nice move," I told her.

As they neared the three-eighths pole, I lowered the binoculars, leaned down and told Mrs. Genter: "If he keeps moving like he is now, we're going to be in the top four for sure if he doesn't get stopped by other horses."

I knew exactly where he'd be when I looked through my binoculars again.

I raised the glasses, focusing them on the spot.

Disbelief!

Shock!

My God, he wasn't there!

In near panic, I swung the glasses to the rear of the field.

What had happened? What had gone wrong?

Unbridled wasn't there.

Numbly, I swung the glasses forward.

Exaltation!

There he was, running with unfettered, ground-eating strides that seemed as effortless as they were powerful.

Unbridled had made such a strong move at the three-eighths pole that he was well ahead of where I expected him to be.

He's only a length off Summer Squall and rolling.

The best part. Craig hasn't even moved on him yet.

It was at this point that I about lost it emotionally in my call of the race for Mrs. Genter.

I see at a glance that we're out of trouble. Unbridled has an open lane to the finish line and that big bay sonofagun has taken dead aim at Summer Squall.

For a split second everything is frozen in time as a thousand things race through a trainer's mind. Victory hangs tantalizingly within reach, but the nerve-shattering fear that it might at the last moment, slip away, retains a firm grip on your emotions.

Is the horse's head coming up? If his head's coming up, it means he's having a breathing problem. No, he's looking good.

Has the jockey uncocked his stick? If he has, it could mean that the horse has already given his all and is fading. Craig isn't moving.

Has the horse switched leads? If he hasn't, it could be another sign of weariness. He switches, the move as smooth as silk.

Is he still on the bit and focused or is he losing steam; his momentum lost? He's on the bit, full of run.

Where are we in relation to the rest of the field? No problem, all but one are behind him.

They're coming down the homestretch.

More than 125,000 voices create a tidal wave of sound.

Craig uncocks his stick.

He's asking Unbridled for more.

Unbridled's nostrils are flared, his eyes wide, ears forward. Adrenaline is pumping.

He gives more.

With a surge of raw power and courage he moves to and passes Summer Squall.

By now I'm about going crazy.

As Unbridled passes Summer Squall, I yell to Mrs. Genter, "He's taking the lead! Mrs. Genter, You're going to win the Kentucky Derby!"

Unbridled sweeps under the wire to win the Kentucky Derby.   *Photo by Dan Johnson*

Then I kept telling her, "There he is, There he is," because directly in front of us was an unimpeded view of about 20 yards of the track. I wanted her to focus on that area so she could see him flash past. Her horse passing beneath the wire.

276

First.

"You've won the Kentucky Derby, Mrs. Genter. . . . I love you!"

The unforgettable moment of the 1990 Kentucky Derby.
ABC Sports

The look of surprise and pure joy on her face as she held her hand over her mouth like a little schoolgirl, is an image that will never fade from my mind.

Unknown to me, all this was being recorded by a camera located somewhere in the area - to this day I don't know where - and my call of the race was being picked up on the microphone placed on me earlier.

As deliriously happy as we were, I had another mission when the race ended. After the Florida Derby, the victory picture was taken before the Genters could get to the winner's circle.

This was not going to happen at the Kentucky Derby.

"Wanda," I said, "you're in charge of getting everyone to

the winner's circle. I'm going to get down there and make sure they don't shoot the picture or make a presentation until everyone is there."

The security folks at Churchill Downs came to the box with a wheelchair because this was the only safe way to get Mrs. Genter through the crowd.

Mrs. Genter said, "I don't know if I should go."

The security men told her: "Just sit in this chair. We'll get you there."

They did.

Two of them picked up the chair and carried her, chair and all, while two more made a pathway through the crowd.

Thanks to their efforts, Mrs. Genter and our entire group of owners and supporters got to the winner's circle for the presentation and the photos.

When the presentation was over, security people escorted Bentley Smith, who is Mrs. Genter's son-in-law, Craig Perret and me to the press box for a news conference.

It was while we were struggling through the crowd that I knew winning the Kentucky Derby would change our lives forever. We would never lead Unbridled, a good racehorse, to the saddling paddock in quite the same way again. No, from now on, he would be Unbridled, winner of the Kentucky Derby.

What happened next that great day was a whirlwind of one interview after another - an unending stream of questions.

Finally, we're back at the barn, at least a partial haven of reality. But even here the surge of recognition and celebrity status, invades.

The phone's answering machine is overloaded. People, some of whom are close friends and others I hadn't seen or talked to in years, are calling from all across the United States and from foreign countries. Included are old friends I'd rodeoed with who want to offer their best wishes and congratulations. They are bursting with pride for one of their own.

It's difficult to explain how winning the Kentucky Derby can change your life. The day before you are training a good racehorse for a fine family and he's only a part, albeit the most important part, of a stable of competitive runners.

That was yesterday. Today, you have the Derby winner and just that quickly, he belongs to everyone.

You drive past restaurants that have signs in the window which read, "Congratulations, Unbridled."

Later, you get on an airplane and people stare and point, then come forward and ask if you're the trainer they saw on TV.

You realize anew that your world can never be quite the same.

Later on Derby Day, as we continued to bask in the beautiful glow of emotions that surged to the surface in the race's aftermath and remained for days, people began telling us about the scene on TV that showed me calling the race and hugging Mrs. Genter.

It was four days before Wanda and I saw the footage. A friend called to say they'd taped it and we should come by and view it for ourselves. The look of pure joy on Mrs. Genter's face brought, and always will bring, a moistness to the eye and a lump to the throat.

Winning the Kentucky Derby is something I wish every trainer and owner could experience.

There's nothing quite like it.

But, if you can't, there still are thrills enough to go around for everyone in this wonderful world of racing.

INDEX